TIM TEBOW

Game Changer:
The Trade to the New York Jets

D0111936

BARBOUR
PUBLISHING

Mike
Yorkey

CONTENTS

Tim has never been afraid to run over or through an opponent. On the field, he is as relentless as Attila the Hun, as unstoppable as a Mack truck plowing through a roadblock. (AP Photo/Phil Sandlin)

INTRODUCTION
HE'S PLAYING WITH PURPOSE
IN THE BIG APPLE

Here we go again.

Tim Tebow, who—according to a *Sports Illustrated* cover headline, "demands that you watch"—finds himself starting all over now that he's donning the hunter-green No. 15 jersey of the New York Jets for the 2012 NFL season.

We all wonder what will transpire—but half the fun of sports is not knowing the outcome. When Tim has the ball in his hands, anything can happen. He certainly grabbed our attention as the biggest football story of 2011, taking the reins of a 1–4 Denver team headed for oblivion and single-handedly spearheading the Broncos to their first AFC West division title in six years—plus an incredible playoff win against the Pittsburgh Steelers.

The Broncos leadership was so thrilled by the turnaround that they went out and signed free agent Peyton Manning to quarterback the team in 2012.

Don't let the door hit you on your way out of town, Tim. But thanks for the memories, especially that sweet pass you threw to Demaryius Thomas against the Steelers.

Now he's taking his act to Broadway, playing in America's biggest city, the epicenter of the media universe. He's always worn his Christian faith on the sleeve of his football jersey, and that won't change in New York. Will the Jets' prickly fans and wise-guy New York media mock him, respect his faith, or just be apathetic? Nobody knows which direction the wind will blow—but it was revealing that Virgin Airlines quickly offered Tim unlimited free flights to London, as long as he remains sexually pure. (A *virgin*, get it?)

Whatever happens in the 2012 season, you can figure that Tim will continue to be one of the most talked-about football players in America. And if he gets a chance to play—or even leap-frogs Mark Sanchez for the starting job—watch out. He'll once again become the most discussed, dissected, and debated athlete on ESPN, the arbiter of what's important in the sports world.

This fishbowl existence has been part of Tim's world since he burst on the scene in 2006 as a true freshman quarterback at the University of Florida. When he's in public, he's a compelling figure who draws stares from bystanders, screams from fans, and clicks from cell phone cameras. He's been called the NFL version of a total solar eclipse, blotting out nearly every other name or topic in the football world.

His smile melts hearts. His demeanor is humble and earnest.

His attitude is respectful to elders and authority figures (like coaches), and his faith moves mountains. His work ethic is off the charts. He's so good-natured and likable that you want to bottle him up and take him home to the family.

Admit it—you can't keep your eyes off him. The camera loves Tim Tebow. His emotions on the field run the gamut: full-throated exhortations to his teammates, fist pumps and bear hugs after big plays and touchdowns, broad smiles and gracious interviews after victories, and emotional on-the-field meetings with youngsters fighting a terminal disease or physical disfigurement.

If football was show business (and, in many ways, that's a good metaphor for a city with Times Square and the Great White Way theater district), Tim's charisma and poise—that special "it"—defines his uniqueness, fortitude, determination, and belief in himself. He has an amazing presence on and off the field as well as a wonderful alliterative roll to his name.

Tim Tebow generates so much heat and attention because his outsized personality broke the mold for the quarterback position during a four-year career at Florida. Things haven't changed since he's been in the NFL. Once he plants his feet under or behind the center, he plays QB like it's his personal fiefdom. He's as relentless as Attila the Hun, as unstoppable as a Mack truck plowing through a roadblock. Now if he could just pass a little better.

His agent, Jimmy Sexton, has predicted that Tim will become the most marketable athlete in history—and that seems more likely now that he's playing for a New York team. Even before he was traded to the Jets, however, the endorsement deals piled up like snowdrifts along Fifth Avenue. Jockey underwear. Nike shoes. FRS energy drinks. During his rookie year with Denver, his No. 15 Broncos jersey led the league in sales in 2010 and was second last season to the forest green jersey belonging to the Green Bay Packers' Aaron Rodgers, another Christian quarterback who's at the top of his game.

"But nobody seems to have popped out quite like Tebow," said Darin David, account director for The Marketing Arm agency.

Everyone wants to be associated with him. Jockey, the underwear company, featured Tim in catalogs and TV and print advertisements because "Jockey's interest in Tim goes beyond football," the company announced. "He is dedicated to community service, and his work ethic, positive attitude, and leadership skills are unquestionable."

Expect more companies like Jockey to launch Tim Tebow campaigns in the future—or maybe we'll see some type of film endeavor. Following the 2011 season, he signed with William Morris Endeavor, one of Hollywood's top talent agencies. WME will be the point for any of Tim's off-the-field pursuits, such as endorsements, books, personal appearances, and any television or movie roles pitched his way.

But don't worry—Tim hasn't gone Hollywood on us. It's not in his DNA or his upbringing.

1
IN THE BEGINNING

Timothy Richard Tebow was born August 14, 1987, in the Philippines.

In a manger.

Because his parents were told there was no room at the inn.

The part about Tim being born in the Philippines is true, but we're just having fun with his "nativity story." But this is the sort of mythmaking that happens when they start calling you "The Chosen One"—in high school.

Tim was born in Makati City, part of metro Manila, because his parents, Bob and Pam Tebow, were living in the Philippines as missionaries at the time. Bob and Pam met at the University of Florida in 1967, when Bob was a sophomore and Pam was a freshman. Even back then, Bob knew his life's goal: to share the message of Jesus Christ with others.

That was certainly a different goal than the one set forth by his father, whom Bob described as a workaholic who moved the family from Alabama to California to Florida as he developed a business in sales and finance. "Growing up, I knew my goal was to get a job and make a million dollars," Bob said.

That desire evaporated during a high school ski trip organized by Young Life, a ministry that reaches out to adolescents. The slopes were bare from warm weather that winter, which kept the Young Life group indoors for presentations and lectures. There, Bob heard the gospel message and became a Christian, a choice that would shape the rest of his life.

When Bob started attending the University of Florida, he and a close friend, Ander Crenshaw (who in 2001 began a career as a member of the U.S. House of Representatives, representing Florida's 4th congressional district) started a Campus Crusade for Christ chapter on the Gainesville campus.

Bob met Pam when he was publicizing a Campus Crusade event. She was the daughter of a U.S. Army colonel who moved frequently, with many of his postings beyond U.S. borders. Pam settled in Tampa during her high school years.

Bob and Pam became friends, and their first date came a year later, when Bob invited Pam to join him at . . . a football game between the University of Florida and the University of Georgia. The rivalry game was played each year at a neutral site: Jacksonville. The Gators won, which may have been a sign of good things to come.

Their love blossomed, and they graduated together from the University of Florida in 1971—he with a degree in health and human performance, and she with a degree from the College of Journalism and Communications. They married that summer and moved to Portland, Oregon, where Bob enrolled at Western Seminary to earn master's degrees in divinity and theology.

The extra schooling took five years. When Bob was finished, he and Pam moved back to Florida, where he became the area representative for the Fellowship of Christian Athletes (FCA) in the northeastern part of the state. Even though Bob had to raise his own support, he and Pam felt financially secure enough to start a family. After their first child, Christy, arrived in 1976, the parents spaced out Katie, Robby, Peter, and the family caboose—Tim—over the next 11 years.

Beginning in 1976, the Tebows started making major moves every three years. After a three-year stint with the FCA (1976–1979), Bob moved into church ministry at Southside Baptist Church in Jacksonville, where he was the associate pastor for three years until 1982. Then, for the next three years, he served as pastor of Cornerstone Community Church, also in Jacksonville.

While at Cornerstone, Bob embarked on a life-changing missionary trip to the Philippines. During the visit, he received what he believed was a summons he could not deny: God was calling him to become a missionary in the Philippines.

Bob and Pam believed then, as they do now, that God had been preparing their hearts for the mission field. Though they had been praying He would open this door, think about how difficult the undertaking must have been for the family, especially Pam: she had three children, ages eight, six, and four, as well as

The Gators had three 13-1 years when Tim played, but the 2007 season was the low point. On January 1, 2008, a 41-35 loss to the Michigan Wolverines in the Florida Citrus Bowl dropped Florida to 9-4 for the season. (AP Photo/Scott A. Miller)

an infant son, Peter, who was born in 1984. To pull up stakes in Jacksonville, where her husband was a respected pastor with a bright career ahead, and resettle the family in a Third World country must have bordered upon the unreal for her.

They would move 12 time zones and almost exactly halfway around the world to Southeast Asia, a 19-hour plane trip that would take her far from the comforts of home. The logistics had to be daunting, the heartbreak of leaving behind friends and family gut-wrenching. They would have to sell most of their personal belongings. But to her credit, Pam never blinked. Living abroad as a young girl had certainly prepared her for this time in their lives. Besides, she was convinced this was God's will for the family, and she was fine with that.

The Tebows settled outside Manila, capital city of the Philippines, and the transition went as smoothly as they dared to hope. Filipinos were being trained as pastors, and countless locals were embracing the Christian faith. The Tebow kids—who had yet to reach their teenage years—acclimated well. "It wasn't always easy, but it was a wonderful time for our family," Pam said. "We learned a lot—you always learn a lot when you [live in] a Third World country."

A year after their arrival, Bob was in a remote village in the mountains in Mindanao, playing *The Jesus Film* on a white sheet that hung between two coconut trees. "I was showing a film and preaching that night," he told *Sports Illustrated*. "I was weeping over the millions of babies being [aborted] in America, and I prayed, 'God, if you give me a son, if you give me Timmy, I'll raise him to be a preacher.'"

The previous sentence is taken word-for-word from a *Sports Illustrated* article that ran in the summer of 2009. Did you notice the editorializing? Writer Austin Murphy and/or the SI editors inserted the word "aborted" in brackets to signify that the magazine was not using the original word Bob said (or, in this case, wrote, because Bob Tebow was responding to questions that had been e-mailed to him).

What do you think Bob originally typed? Since he is ardently pro-life, you have to figure he tapped out this sentence on his computer screen:

I was weeping over the millions of babies being killed in America. . .

That's how strongly he—and Pam—felt about abortion, which stops a beating heart and ends the life of a growing human being. Their hearts wept at the carnage of 4,000 abortions that happen every day—1.5 million each year—in the United States.

Sports Illustrated—and the Tebows would tell you the world feels the same way—didn't like the starkness or the reality of the word *killed*. So they chose to insert *aborted* instead. More clinical. Easier to brush off, sweep under the rug.

And then Pam got pregnant with Tim, and she and Bob suddenly had to confront their beliefs about the sanctity of life and the sovereignty of Almighty God.

A CHOICE

When Pam became pregnant with Tim, she was 37 years old, living 9,000 miles from home, the mother of four energetic children, and the wife of a missionary pastor.

The pregnancy was not unexpected. In fact, she and Bob very much desired to have a fifth child. They had been praying for Timmy by name—to this day, they still call him "Timmy," not "Tim"—before she conceived. They wanted to name their son after the young church leader named Timothy, who received a pair of letters from the apostle Paul that now appear in the New Testament.

Just before she became pregnant, however, Pam contracted amoebic dysentery, a disease caused by bacteria transmitted through contaminated drinking water. Dysentery is common in developing and tropical countries like the Philippines and is not to be taken lightly—between 40,000 and 100,000 people die worldwide each year of amoebic dysentery. The disease causes inflammation of the intestines and bloody, severe diarrhea. Dysentery was the leading cause of death in the Philippines.

Pam fell into a coma and was treated aggressively with a series of strong antimicrobial drugs. As she came out of the coma and her condition stabilized, she continued to take the powerful medications.

Then, when she took a pregnancy test, the stick turned blue.

Pam recalled reading a label on her prescription warning that the antimicrobial drug could cause "severe birth defects." She immediately discontinued the treatment protocol, fearing harm had already been done to the life growing inside her. When she told her doctor what had transpired, her worst fears were confirmed—she heard that her "fetus" had been irreversibly damaged. That being the case, the doctor recommended that she "discontinue" the pregnancy—in other words, have an abortion.

Actually, "They didn't recommend," Pam said. "They didn't really give me a choice. That was the only option they gave me."

To Pam and Bob, there was a lot more than a "fetus" growing inside her womb. This was a life, not a glob of tissue or a "product" of conception. Since the Tebows believed God was the author of life—and death—there was no doubt in their minds that they would trust Him in this perilous situation for both Pam *and* the unborn child.

Pam and Bob's decision was set in concrete, and their determination to see the pregnancy through didn't waver when Pam's doctor said that her placenta had detached from the uterine wall—a dangerous development known as placental abruption. Pam was a high-risk patient living in the Philippine countryside, and a severe condition like this one could have easily killed her. Once again, she was counseled to abort—to save her own life. Certainly she would be justified in taking this measure. But Pam wouldn't consider it.

"We were determined to trust the Lord with the children He would give us," she said in an interview with Focus on the Family president Jim Daly, taped after she and Tim completed filming their Super Bowl commercial in 2010. "And if God called me to give up my life, then He would take care of my family."

Bottom line: Pam Tebow wasn't just *willing* to risk her life for Timmy; she actually *chose* to risk her life so her son might live.

At the seventh month of her crisis pregnancy, Pam traveled

to Manila, where she went on bed rest and received around-the-clock care from an American-trained physician. It was a touch-and-go pregnancy the entire way, and she and Bob prayed earnestly that God would give them the chance to raise the son they would name Timmy.

On her due date, August 14, Pam gave birth to Tim—and the family learned just how serious the placental abruption had been. "There was a great big clump of blood that came out where the placenta wasn't properly attached, basically for the whole nine months," Bob said in an interview with Focus on the Family. "He was a miracle baby."

He was also skinny and long—like the malnourished new-born he was. The Tebows asked friends and family to pray that their newborn son would grow up big and strong. "It was amazing that God spared him, but we knew God had His hand on his life," Bob said. "We all, through the years, have told Timmy that."

2
BACK IN THE USA

When Tim was three years old, the Tebows decided to move back to Florida, closer to home and family. After laying a strong foundation and sending pastors out into the fields, Bob felt he could run the Bob Tebow Evangelistic Association from a distance while making periodic trips to the western Pacific. He could also better organize short-term and summer mission trips to the Philippines while living stateside.

The family moved back to the Jacksonville area, to a 44-acre farm tucked between the city and the tranquil setting of Baldwin. When Tim was a kindergartner, he joined his four older sisters and brothers at a special school with a limited enrollment—the Tebow Homeschool.

Homeschooling was becoming better known to the general public in the 1980s, thanks to pioneers like Dr. Raymond Moore and his wife, Dorothy—educators who became vocal advocates

After winning the 2008 BCS National Championship against Oklahoma, Tim and the Florida team greeted 42,000 Gators fans at The Swamp. "Let's do it again!" he exclaimed, saying he would return for his senior year at Florida. (AP Photo/Phil Sandlin)

for homeschooling, particularly among Christian families. Parents purchased curriculum packages and teaching aids geared to their children's ages. The Tebows were early adopters, beginning in 1982 with Christy.

Let's face it: homeschooling was a radical idea back then, and it's still looked upon in many circles as strange. How can children learn enough to get a good education or get into college if they don't receive instruction from trained teachers in public and private school classrooms?

The Tebows had some clear ideas about how they wanted to raise their children. They were wary of worldly influences intruding upon their five offspring—outside influences that would smack them the moment they stepped on the school bus. They were also greatly concerned about the moral and cultural values conveyed in the public school classrooms.

So Bob and Pam sought a different approach. They wanted to inspire their children to love God, live excellently, be humble, and serve their fellow man. As hands-on parents who would alone be responsible for their children's formal educations, they would closely monitor what came into the home and be intentional about the lessons their children would learn.

"If I could get my kids to the age of 25 and they knew God and served God and had character qualities that pleased God, then I knew God would be happy and I would be happy," Bob said. "The only way I could do that was to do it myself, commit to God that this is my job. Traditional academics had to take a backseat to God's Word and character-building."

They started homeschooling Christy, Katie, Robby, and Peter before the family moved to the Philippines. Pam taught them the Three R's—reading, 'riting, and 'rithmetic—plus other subjects as they got older. Everything their children learned would be taught through the prism of the Bible, with an emphasis on learning how to speak in public. Bob and Pam wanted each of their children to feel comfortable and confident in communicating their beliefs.

Memorizing Bible verses, as well as life lessons, were foundational to learning in the Tebow home. For instance, Proverbs 27:2 (New King James Version) taught the children not to brag on themselves:

> *Let another man praise you, and not your own mouth;*
> *A stranger, and not your own lips.*

Bob and Pam believed humility was one of the greatest measures of a person's character, so they constantly had their children memorize Bible verses on humility, such as:

- Remember how the LORD your God led you all the way in the desert these forty years, to humble you and to test you in order to know what was in your heart, whether or not you would keep his commands (Deuteronomy 8:2).
- You save the humble, but your eyes are on the haughty to bring them low (2 Samuel 22:28).

- When pride comes, then comes disgrace, but with humility comes wisdom (Proverbs 11:2).
- The fear of the LORD teaches a man wisdom, and humility comes before honor (Proverbs 15:33).
- Humility and the fear of the LORD bring wealth and honor and life (Proverbs 22:4).

When the children weren't memorizing Bible verses or doing schoolwork, they learned discipline through chores like taking out the trash, vacuuming, making their beds, and washing dishes. That was just the beginning, since there was always work to do on such a large property dotted with pines and grassy fields—mowing the grass, building fences, feeding the cows.

The parents turned a half-acre plot behind the house into a vegetable garden, and the children learned the value of stoop labor. They weeded with hoes and planted and cared for the vegetables that fed their family of seven year-round. They slaughtered and ate the cows they raised. Bucking fallen trees in the "back 40" was another way Bob instilled the value of physical labor in his sons.

Bob and Pam had a firm rule in the Tebow household: no complaining. That rule must have stuck because you can't call Tim Tebow a grumbler or whiner today. The characteristic has shown itself on the football field. While Tim deeply hates losing at anything, he's never been one to offer excuses.

NO GRAND PLAN

It's a great quip, a superb sound bite, and something Bob Tebow has repeated many times over the years. It goes like this:

"I asked God for a preacher, and He gave me a quarterback."

There was no grand plan in the Tebow family to raise a great athlete, let alone a star quarterback who would become an NFL starter. In the Tebow household, sports were low-key. They had to be, if you think about it. During their five years in the Philippines, there was no such thing as Little League or AYSO soccer for Tim's older brothers and sisters. The kids played outside, ran around, did things that kids do. But there were no "travel teams" in the Philippines.

After the Tebow family returned to Florida, Christy played some tennis, and Katie was a runner. Tim's older brothers Robby and Peter got into youth baseball and football. The parents kept everything in perspective; they knew getting exercise was good for the body, but they didn't want their schedules revolving around sports. The Tebows *were* into competition, though. "There was no mercy in our family," Bob said. "Katie, every once in a while, would show you mercy, but everyone else would cut your throat."

The Tebow family's competitive streak extended beyond sports. Board games like Monopoly quickly deteriorated into overheated emotions when a simple roll of the dice landed one of the Tebow kids on Boardwalk or Park Place teeming with red hotels. And woe to the Risk players when their territories were captured. When Bob taught each of his children how to play

At the University of the Florida, Tim was a juggernaut who could beat opponents with his arm or his legs. Big and broad-shouldered, he broke the mold for the quarterback and dominated the field. (AP Photo/John Raoux)

chess, the sparks would fly following a checkmate.

Bob said he never let any of the children beat him at chess—and no one can topple his king to this day. The last time he challenged anyone to take him on, there were no takers. "It's pretty dog-eat-dog around here," he said. "They know the outcome."

With that thought in mind, Bob noticed something about Tim, even when his son was a five-year-old: he had a tremendous arm and impressive hand-eye coordination—as well as the Tebow competitive streak. Tim threw left-handed, but that was his natural side, so Bob didn't try to change him.

Tim could throw a football with excellent velocity for a pint-sized tyke, and when he had a bat in his hand, he could swing and hit the ball squarely. His parents thought he'd have fun playing T-ball, the pressureless entry point for youth baseball, so they signed him up. There's no live pitching in T-ball; each batter steps up to the plate and swings at a ball placed on a plastic tee. Once the player hits the ball into fair territory, he starts running.

Many five-year-olds are clueless about how baseball is played, and some prefer to lie down in the outfield and watch the clouds roll by. Not Tim, who played second base for the White Sox. If he had another gift besides pure athleticism, it was awareness of his surroundings. He would get perturbed when the other kids didn't know what was going on, as Guerry Smith described on Rivals.com:

Some of his teammates were picking at the ground without even paying attention. *How is that possible?* he wondered.

There's a game going on. Focus on the game. He heard players say they were out there for the snow cone they would get when the game was over. Not Tebow. The competition was all that mattered at the moment. He heard his coach say, "You don't have to play to win. Just play to have fun," and he could not comprehend the mindset. *It's not fun if you don't win*, he said to himself. He was dumbfounded. He was also five years old.

Tim also played Pop Warner football. As one of the bigger kids on the team, he played tight end on offense and linebacker on defense. Then one day, when he was 11 years old, his coach, David Hess, watched him practice and said to himself, *This kid is such a talented athlete. He'd make a good quarterback.*

Hess asked Tim to get down on one knee and throw the ball as far as he could. The youngster heaved the ball 30 yards in the air. After that, Tim was lining up behind center. "Guess that's my claim to fame," Coach Hess said years later.

People who knew Tim during his Pop Warner days are still telling Tebow stories—like the time he lined up behind center on his team's 20-yard line and saw the tackles cheating a bit. Instead of taking the snap and tossing the ball to the tailback—the play called in the huddle—Tim ran a quarterback sneak . . . all the way into the end zone, 80 yards away.

When Tim wasn't flying past defenders, he was running over players who dared get in his way. Linebackers who searched for Tim in the open field to deliver a hit stopped searching after the first time they collided with him.

Then there was the tremendous arm strength his father first saw back on the farm. Tim was heaving the ball 50 yards in the air as a sixth grader, and everyone who saw him throw thought, *Wait until he gets to high school.*

Except Tim was homeschooled. How was he going to play high school football when he wasn't even going to *go* to high school?

3
LOOKING UP TO A HERO

When he was young, Tim's parents encouraged him to pick a hero who modeled humility and modesty. They suggested just the person for the nine-year-old to emulate: Danny Wuerffel, the University of Florida quarterback who would win the Heisman Trophy in 1996 and lead the Gators to a national championship the same season.

Dad and Mom both graduated from the University of Florida, so the Tebows were Gator fans who occasionally attended some games. Older sister Katie was making plans to enroll there in the fall of 1997. Tim, who slept under a Gator bedspread and had a bathroom that sported a Gator shower curtain, tacked a giant color poster of Danny Wuerffel to his bedroom wall. Before the start of the 1996 season, young Tim enjoyed seeing his hero at Gators Fan Day.

Tim liked how the Florida QB was quick to give God credit

Tim was part of two national championship teams during his four-year career at the University of Florida. Here, Tim celebrates with Florida head coach Urban Meyer after winning the SEC conference championship over Alabama. A month later, the Gators were crowned national champs after defeating the Oklahoma Sooners.
(AP Photo/Dave Martin)

and living his life to bring honor to Him. Danny loved quoting Proverbs 3:5–6 to the media: "Trust in the Lord with all your heart and lean not on your own understanding; in all your ways acknowledge him, and he will make your paths straight."

So Tim wanted to be like Danny Wuerffel—and to play quarterback like him. Would he get his chance?

The answer was yes, thanks to a new Florida law that allowed homeschooled children to take part in interscholastic sports. A homeschooling mom named Brenda Dickinson spearheaded a two-year battle in the Florida legislature that ended in 1996 with the passage of a law providing home-educated students with the opportunity to participate on athletic teams at their local schools. In other words, if a child was schooled at home, he or she had to be "accommodated" and couldn't be kept off the interscholastic playing field.

Florida became one of 16 states that allowed homeschooled kids to play varsity sports at a traditional high school. Robby and Peter Tebow took advantage of that opportunity and played high school football at Trinity Christian Academy in Jacksonville, a K–12 school with 450 high school students.

When Tim reached ninth grade, he was itching to play at Trinity as well. But Tim didn't start out playing quarterback. The Trinity Christian coach, Verlon Dorminey, looked at Tim's broad-shouldered build and lined him up on the varsity team at tight end on offense and linebacker on defense.

That was okay for his freshman year, but Tim wanted to play quarterback. Quarterbacks were the playmakers, the center of action. If you were going to *beat* the other team, you needed a quarterback who could make plays. Tim wanted to *lead* his team to victory, not depend on someone else making plays.

Coach Dorminey was open to the idea, but he had installed a Wing-T offense that relied heavily on the run. In his system, the quarterback made a lot of handoffs or ran off the option play. Little or no passing. This run-centered offense worked for Dorminey and the team: Trinity Christian won the Florida state championship in its division in 2002.

That's not what Bob Tebow wanted for his son, though. He knew Tim had a special gift for throwing the ball and that he needed to be on a team where he could shine as quarterback. He didn't want his son typecast at tight end or linebacker—grunt positions that take size. Quarterback—the position with the ultimate skill set—was where he needed to be.

If Tim was ever going to play quarterback in high school, he had to make his move. That's because quarterbacks establish themselves on the varsity team during their sophomore seasons. Maybe they don't play that much because a senior or a junior is ahead of them—but they take their place on the depth chart and learn the position on the practice field.

Since Trinity Christian didn't throw the ball—and since Tim didn't go to school there anyway—the Tebows starting shopping around. They found a public high school in nearby St. John's County where the coach, Craig Howard, ran a spread offense and liked to see the ball in the air.

The school was Nease High, and the football team hadn't

been winning much. In fact, the Panthers were 2–8 the season before Tim arrived, 1–9 the year before that.

In other words, the perfect situation for Tim Tebow.

"We wanted to give Tim the opportunity to develop his God-given talent and to achieve his lifelong dream of playing quarterback," Bob said. "It wasn't that we were leaving an unsuccessful program to go to a successful one; it was the other way around."

There was one hitch, though: Tim had to live in the Nease High School district. The Tebow farm was situated in nearby Duval County.

The Tebows overcame that hurdle by renting an apartment close to Nease High in Ponte Vedra Beach. They put the family farm up for sale and signed up Tim to play football at Nease High. Pam and Tim did Bible studies and worked through his home school curriculum in the morning and early afternoon, then it was off to football practice at Nease High. The family farm never sold, so the Tebows eventually kept their homestead. But as Bob said, "We were willing to make that sacrifice. We made sacrifices for all our children."

Nease High—named after Allen Duncan Nease, a pioneer of Florida's reforestation and conservation efforts in the mid-twentieth century—was a public high school of about 1,600 students that played in Florida's 4A division. In Florida—a hotbed of high school football talent—schools competed in one of eight classifications, all based on enrollment. The largest classification in the state was 6A, and the smallest was 1B, so there were some schools in Florida classed higher than Nease and many classed lower.

Tim's talent could not be denied nor his work ethic overlooked. Coach Howard certainly noticed. "People can always lead with words but not always with actions," he said. "Timmy was the hardest worker I've ever been around. His work ethic was uncompromising, and all of those around him were affected by it."

Tim won the starting quarterback role in his sophomore season. Based on their history of losing, though, the Panthers figured to be the patsy on other teams' schedules. "We had six road games my sophomore year, and we were the homecoming game for all six of them," Tim said. "Talk about embarrassing."

But the Panthers, with their sophomore quarterback making throws, bullying his way through the line, and never giving up, acquitted themselves well during Tim's first season. Nease High finished 5–5 in 2003, a turnaround that portended better things to come.

BREAKOUT TIME

Tim had a big junior season in high school football. He enjoyed a strong cast around him to block, catch the ball, and stop the other team from scoring. In that respect, he was in the right place at the right time.

But Tim didn't go to school with his teammates. No friendly banter between classes or hanging out in the cafeteria during lunchtime. No horseplay or kidding around while gathering for a school assembly.

Yet Tim won over his teammates with his hard work on the practice field, his unyielding determination to win, and his

Dramatic shots like this show you why the camera loves Tim Tebow: His full-throated exhortations to his teammates led Florida to two national championships while Tim played there. (AP Photo/ Mark Humphrey)

respectful attitude toward players and coaches. His teammates saw him as a nice, fun-loving guy—as one of them, even though he didn't go to classes during the school day.

For Tim, all the pieces were in place for a successful 2004 season. He was big and brawny, pushing past 6 feet, 2 inches tall, and weighing in north of 215 pounds. He single-handedly, by force of will and great talent, took a nothing team and turned it into an 11–2 powerhouse that advanced to the third round of the state playoffs.

If Tim wasn't pile-driving his way through the line like a determined fullback, he was hitting receivers between the numbers and lofting bombs into the end zone. Suddenly, rival schools didn't want anything to do with Nease High on homecoming night.

Coach Howard saw that he had a thoroughbred in Tim, and he let him run—and throw and throw and throw. Before the season was over, Tim had set the state record for total yards in a season with 5,576—of which 4,304 yards came from passing, for an average of 331 yards per game. He was also responsible for *70* touchdowns in 13 games—and that's not a typo: he tossed 46 touchdown passes (more than three per game) and ran for 24 more, making himself the ultimate "dual-threat" quarterback. He threw just six interceptions all season.

NO FACE IN THE CROWD

The honors rolled in for Tim Tebow following his junior season: Florida Dairy Farmers Player of the Year, All-State, and a third-place finish in Florida's Mr. Football balloting. He rose up the college recruiting Web sites such as Rivals.com and SuperPrep.com like a hit song on a Top 40 chart. Scout.com even ranked him third nationally among high school quarterback prospects.

Sportswriter John Patton of the *Gainesville Sun* called Tim "the best high school football player I have ever seen"—even though he still had another season of high school ball left. Then, at the end of his junior season, *Sports Illustrated* printed his smiling mug in the magazine's "Faces in the Crowd" section.

The hype machine was pulling out of the driveway.

College coaches descended upon the Tebow family like solicitous salesmen carrying briefcases filled with wares. Eighty schools offered him scholarships and pleaded with him to come play for State U—but the only ones the Tebows actively considered were Miami, Michigan, Southern California, Alabama, and Bob and Pam's alma mater—the University of Florida.

But the Tebow parents didn't want Tim to make a verbal commitment to any college at the end of his junior year. They weren't ready yet; they wanted to take their time.

As word got around about this Tebow kid in Florida, an ESPN producer smelled a good story and sent a camera crew from Murrah Communications to Nease High during the summer of 2005. Coach Howard gave the film crew full access throughout the 2005 season—training camp, locker room, practice field, and the sidelines during the games. The coach even allowed himself to be miked.

This would be an ESPN *Faces in Sports* program, and the title of the hour-long documentary was *The Chosen One*. The storyline was Tim's record-setting career at Nease, his senior season, and the team's drive toward a state championship. The program ended with Tim's postseason announcement in December of which school he had chosen to attend.

The Chosen One is still worth watching. (It's readily available in five segments on YouTube.) It's a chance to watch a youthful Tim—wearing a No. 5 jersey—not only develop as a player but also into a young man learning to deal with intense media scrutiny. He handled everything with aplomb. There are many amazing scenes:

- Tim and his dad sitting at the dinner table in their ranch house, sifting through a mound of recruiting letters from the nation's top college football coaches—many handwritten—informing Tim that he'd be a "welcome addition" to their program.
- Pam perched at a small table with Tim in their Ponte Vedra apartment, working through a home school lesson together.
- Bob and Pam talking about their years in the Philippines and a clip of Tim preaching before hundreds of Filipino kids when he was only 15 years old.
- Tim in the locker room, firing up his team before a big game like it was the end of the world.
- Tim suffering a broken leg but refusing to be pulled

out of the game, and later hobbling 29 yards into the end zone on sheer guts.

- Bob standing in a grassy field, reading Proverbs 22:6 from his Bible ("Train a child in the way he should go . . .").

THE NEXT BIG THING

The cameras were there when Nease High opened the 2005 season with a road game against highly regarded Hoover High in Hoover, Alabama, which aired *nationally* on ESPN. Even though Nease lost 50–29, everyone agreed that Tim put on quite a show.

The national media had now officially anointed Tim as the Next Big Thing. Tim backed that up by putting together another record-breaking season and leading Nease to its first state championship, which the Panthers took home after beating Armwood High 44–37 in the state final. Tim's stats: 237 yards and four touchdowns in the air, 153 yards and two touchdowns on the ground . . . and jokes about selling popcorn at halftime.

All that was left for Tim to do was to announce which college had won his heart. The family narrowed down the choices to Alabama or Florida, then Bob and Pam stepped aside. *It's your decision, son. You're the one who's going to be playing there. You pray about it and let the Lord guide your steps.*

Three days after pocketing the state championship, Tim—dressed in a dark coat, blue shirt, and white tie—took the podium at the Nease High Performing Arts Center. He stood before an auditorium packed with hundreds of screaming teenagers and

They call it "three-second evangelism"—Tim's clever idea of putting Bible verses on his swatches of "eye black." Tim started the practice during the 2008 season by putting PHL on the black strip under his right eye and 4:13 under the left eye. (AP Photo/Phil Sandlin)

Gator partisans. ESPN's cameras were there—live.

That morning, Tim and his golden lab, Otis, had gone for a long walk among the pine trees and oaks that outlined their homestead. He sat next to a lake and thought and prayed about what he should do. He and his parents liked both coaches; Urban Meyer at Florida and Mike Shula at Alabama were God-fearing men of strong character. Both schools were capable of winning the national title. This was one of those win-win decisions.

In the end, the edge went to Florida. Coach Meyer ran a spread offense, just like Coach Howard did at Nease, and the family's deep roots at the University of Florida couldn't be glossed over. Mom and Dad went there, and Pam's father had played basketball there. Tim had grown up in Gator Nation. The school was close to home, which meant his parents and siblings—Team Tebow—could watch him play at Ben Hill Griffin Stadium, also known as "The Swamp."

Bob and Pam held their breath as Tim straddled the podium, looked straight into the camera, and said, "I will be playing college football next year at the University of Florida."

4
THE GREEN SHIRT
AT GATOR NATION

How do you describe the four-year college career that launched Tebowmania and lifted Tim into the living rooms of millions of Americans?

Do you start with Tim's freshman year and his double-pump "jump pass" for a one-yard touchdown against LSU that had announcers raving about his originality? Or was it the *Braveheart* scene at Florida State—when Tim's face and white jersey were smeared in reddish "war paint" from the end zone? Or how about the controversy when he started inscribing Bible verses on his eye black?

When Tim announced, "I will be playing college football next year at the University of Florida," he was talking about playing the very *next* season, not kicking back and enjoy a low-stress redshirt year. In January 2006, within a few weeks of his announcement, Tim enrolled at Florida. He didn't have to wait to graduate with his high school class—he *was* the class.

Tim was eligible to enroll in college because he had completed his studies and had taken an SAT test in ninth grade. By becoming a University of Florida student, Tim made himself eligible to participate in spring football practice—the rehearsal time for the fall season.

In the college football lexicon, he was not a red shirt but a "green shirt"—green as in "go early." A green-shirt athlete is someone who graduates from high school in December of his senior year and immediate enrolls in college so he can participate in spring practice—and get a head start on learning the system and moving up the depth chart.

Chris Leak was a senior and a three-year starter for the Gators, so he was the No. 1 quarterback. But Tim wasn't willing to rock on his cleats on the Florida sidelines, helmet in hand, waiting for his chance to play. He was going to *compete* for the job, even as a true freshman.

At the annual Orange and Blue scrimmage game, which ended three weeks of spring practice, Tim looked sharp in leading his Orange team to a 24–6 victory. "Chris Leak is our quarterback, and Tim Tebow is a guy who is going to play," Coach Meyer said afterward. "There is no quarterback controversy. There are two great young men who we are going to build an offense around to be successful."

Translation: *We're going to start Chris Leak so our freshman quarterback doesn't have the pressure of being the starter, but he's going to be playing a lot.*

Tim did play a lot as a true freshman in 2006, even though Florida had arguably the toughest schedule in the nation. He scored the first time he touched the ball in a Florida uniform—on a goal-line keeper against Southern Mississippi. Coach Meyer continued to play Tim in spot situations, bringing him along slowly. But in the third game of the season, against Tennessee—in Knoxville, before 106,818 rabid Volunteer fans—Meyer threw Tim into the fire. In the fourth quarter, with the Gators trailing by six points, Florida faced a fourth-and-one inside Tennessee territory. Meyer flung Tim into the game, Tim punched out two yards to keep the drive alive, and Chris Leak took his place and led the Gators to the winning score.

Against Southeastern Conference opponents, Florida fell into a familiar pattern throughout the season—fall behind early, then claw its way back. Against LSU, Tim unveiled his first "jump pass." With Florida knocking on the door at the one-yard line, Tim took the snap five yards behind center, ran toward the pile, then suddenly leaped and lobbed a rainbow pass to his tight end, Tate Casey. Touchdown!

It was a clever gadget play—known in the Florida playbook as Trey Left, 341 Stop Bend X Fake—that hadn't been seen since the days of Bronko Nagurski and leather helmets. With retro panache, Tim would make two more jump passes in his career at Florida.

After defeating LSU, Florida—now ranked No. 2 in the country—suffered its first hiccup of the season—against Auburn

It was a lot of fun to be a Florida Gator when Tim Tebow was around. During his stellar four-year career (2006-2009), Florida was 48-7. Here he's pictured with backup quarterback John Brantley. (AP Photo/Phil Sandlin, File)

in a 27–17 road loss in an ESPN *GameDay* match-up. A controversial fourth-quarter fumble by Chris Leak, with Florida trailing 21–17 but driving for the potential win, sealed the Gators' fate.

That was the only smudge on an otherwise golden 2006 Florida football season. The Gators ran the table the rest of the way, beating Georgia, Florida State, and Arkansas (in the SEC Championship Game) to climb back to No. 2 in the polls and into the BCS National Championship Game—played at the new University of Phoenix Stadium in Glendale, Arizona—against top-ranked Ohio State.

Florida thrashed the Buckeyes 41–14 to win its second national football championship in school history—the other one happening in 1996 when Danny Wuerffel was the Gator quarterback. The victory also helped mark the first time in college sports history that the NCAA college basketball and football titles rested in the same trophy case—the Gator men's basketball team having won the national championship in the spring of 2006. Chris Leak played clutch football, and when Tim spelled him, he found the soft spots in the Ohio State defense with his power running, scoring one touchdown and throwing for another on college football's biggest night.

At a well-attended victory celebration at Ben Hill Griffin Stadium a few days later, a special guest was invited onstage to hand Chris Leak the Most Valuable Player trophy. Who was the surprise invitee?

Danny Wuerffel, Tim's boyhood hero.

After telling Chris they were now the only starting Gator

quarterbacks in Florida football history to wear national championship rings, Danny paused for a moment and turned to the freshman quarterback standing nearby. Everyone wondered what Danny Wonderful would say.

"There's room for another one next year, Timmy Tebow," he said.

The baton had been officially passed.

IT'S TIM'S TEAM NOW

With Chris Leak graduated, the Florida Gators were now Tim Tebow's team. Everyone knew it. A FLORIDA FOLK HERO PREPARES TO FACE REALITY read a preseason headline in the *New York Times,* which knew an important story when it saw one.

The story noted that during the offseason, Tim had sung "She Thinks My Tractor's Sexy" onstage with country singer Kenny Chesney, preached in two prisons "so convincingly" that 200 hardened criminals began weeping and became Christians, and dealt with coeds camping outside his apartment—some who asked him to autograph their underwear.

Saying that Tim had a big year in 2007, after having just turned 19, would be like saying the New York Yankees and Murderer's Row had a big year in 1927. In the season opener against Western Kentucky, Tim led the Gators to touchdowns on their first four possessions. He finished his first career start by going 13-for-17 for 300 yards with three touchdown passes and one rushing touchdown in a 49–3 wipeout. Another warm-up game against Troy was also a Tebow gem.

Tim's first big test was the 2007 SEC opener against Tennessee, which was played before 90,707 hot and sticky fans at The Swamp. Tim was unstoppable, running and throwing the ball up and down the field almost at will. When he scored on a seven-yard touchdown run in the second quarter, CBS cameras caught safety and roommate Tony Joiner planting a kiss on Tim's left cheek as a reward.

The lovefest continued until Tim's first interception of the season, which resulted in a 93-yard Volunteer touchdown to pull Tennessee to within 28–20 in the third quarter. After that, though, the rout was on—31 unanswered Florida points as Tim racked up 61 yards on the ground and 299 yards through the air.

HE15MAN TIME

This amalgamation of Joe Montana and Jim Brown added up to two words: *Tebow hysteria.* Some zealous Florida fans created TimTebowFacts.com, where fans could contribute a list of Tim's most legendary, Paul Bunyanesque accomplishments. T-shirt makers started silk-screening "He15man" on Gator blue shirts, and the ESPN and CBS football pundits declared that Tim was the early-season favorite for the Heisman Trophy, even though they were careful to insert a "but"—*but a sophomore has never won the Heisman, Lou.* They pointed out that ex-Gator quarterback Rex Grossman didn't win one in 2001 and running back Darren McFadden of Arkansas didn't pick up the Heisman in 2006, even though both players had superb seasons—so it was likely never to happen.

Tim's legend expanded the following week against Ole Miss when he took over a road game in Oxford, Mississippi, that Florida looked destined to lose. The Gators struggled most of the game until five consecutive Tebow runs set up a short field goal that gave the Gators a 30–24 lead with less than five minutes to play. After a stop, when Florida needed to run time off the clock, Tim carried the ball six consecutive times to secure a victory and keep the No. 3 Gators undefeated for the season. In all, Tim accounted for all four Gator touchdowns and 427 of his team's 507 total yards.

But the Gators lost three of their next four games, falling to Auburn at home, LSU in Baton Rouge, and Georgia at the neutral Jacksonville site. Tim didn't do much against Georgia because of a right shoulder contusion he suffered the previous week against Kentucky. When he was in the game, the Georgia rush menaced him the entire afternoon, sacking him six times. It seemed like he was running for his life the entire game.

Tim, who had wiped tears from his face after walking off the field at LSU, had to fight back moisture in his eyes at the postgame podium as he faced the media following the tough loss to interstate rival Georgia. "I do take them [the losses] hard," he said, "but that's because I am so passionate."

Listening to the Georgia game on her computer, via the Internet, was his sister Christy. It was the middle of the night in Bangladesh, where she had recently moved with her husband, Joey, and their one-year-old daughter, Claire, to do missionary work.

After the game, Tim spoke by phone with Christy, who told him how she and her family were adjusting to life in one of the poorest countries of the world. He felt chastened. "It makes you realize that everything that happens in this game doesn't really mean that much in the grand scheme of things," Tim said. "Losing to Georgia is not the biggest thing in the world."

The Gators—and Tim—bounced back and played a perfect November, even though his shoulder bruise still bothered him. He shook off the pain and ran for five touchdowns against South Carolina, set a career-best in passing yards with 338 against Florida Atlantic, and dominated intrastate rival Florida State at The Swamp, despite suffering a displaced fracture on his non-throwing right hand. He played 30 downs with the busted hand and laid out his final argument to win the Heisman Trophy. In the closing moments of a one-sided 45–12 victory against the Seminoles, Gator cheerleaders struck Heisman poses—carriage slightly bent, leg up, right arms thrust out to stiff-arm a tackler—on the sidelines.

Florida finished the season a respectable 9–3 and earned a January 1, 2008, date with Michigan at the Citrus Bowl. But the big story in Gator Nation was whether Tim would capture the Heisman Trophy.

In the 72-year history of the award, Heisman voters—sportswriters and past winners—had never handed the award to a sophomore, reserving the honor for upperclassmen. It seemed to be one of those unwritten rules.

Wait your turn, son.

But who had played better than Tim Tebow in 2007? Some said Arkansas running back Darren McFadden deserved it after failing to strike the pose in 2006, or that University of Hawaii senior quarterback Colt Brennan should win because of his outlandish passing stats—but no one played better than Tim in 2007.

In early December, Tim and his family flew to New York City for the Heisman Trophy ceremony at the Nokia Theatre in Times Square. It turned out to be a family reunion when Christy and her family flew to New York from Bangladesh.

When he heard his name announced as the winner, a beaming Tim sprang out of his chair and hugged his parents, then Gator coach Urban Meyer. Standing on the stage with all the surviving Heisman winners since 1935 was his boyhood idol, Danny Wuerffel, who greeted him with another hug.

After first thanking God for the ability to play football, Tim thanked his teammates back home, his coaches, and especially his parents: "I want to thank my dad, who taught me a work ethic every day growing up, and my mom, who instilled in me so many great characters."

*It's okay, Tim. This was live TV before millions of viewers. We know what you meant: Mom instilled in you so many great charac-*teristics.

Football commentators agreed that being the first NCAA Division 1 quarterback ever to have a "20/20" season—22 rushing touchdowns and 29 touchdown passes—sealed the deal with Heisman voters. Tim, the youngest Heisman winner ever at 20

No sophomore had ever won the Heisman Trophy—given annually to college football's best player—until Tim came along. He received the prestigious award in New York City at the end of the 2007 regular season. (AP Photo/Julie Jacobson)

years of age, accepted the trophy with a blue cast on his right hand.

The 2007 season ended with a 41–35 loss to Michigan on New Year's Day. Tim played with a soft cast to protect his mending right hand. Although the defeat was disappointing to the Gators and their fans, they knew Tim would return the following season—all healed up and with a talented, more experienced team surrounding him.

Deep within, a passion burned within Tim for a national championship ring—the one Danny Wuerffel said there was room for.

5
PROMISE MADE, PROMISE KEPT

In Gator lore, it's called "The Promise."

Here's the situation. Through the first three games of the 2008 season, Florida was pancaking opponents. Victories over Hawaii, Miami, and Tennessee were as lopsided as some girls' basketball games. The talk in Gator Nation was that this team could go undefeated—something never before done in the history of Florida football.

Ole Miss was coming to Gainesville a decided underdog—22 points according to the oddsmakers. Quarterbacking the Rebels was Jevan Snead, who (1) "decommitted" to Florida after Tim announced he would become a Gator and (2) enrolled at Texas but transferred to Ole Miss after getting beat out by Colt McCoy. So you could excuse Snead if he had a bit of an inferiority complex playing in Tim Tebow's house.

But Snead was a gamer, as was the entire Rebel team. They made plays, recovered fumbles from Tim and star running back Percy Harvin, and "hung around"—football-speak for a team that should have been put away after falling behind 17–7.

The game was tied 24–24 midway through the fourth quarter when the Rebels—playing with house money since they were still in the game—got lucky (if you're a Gator fan) or made a great effort (if you're an Ole Miss fan). Snead found Shay Hodge all alone on the sideline for an 86-yard scoring play to give Ole Miss a 31–24 lead with 5:26 to play.

Tim and the Gators hitched up their pants and scored quickly when Percy Harvin scooted 15 yards for a touchdown. The extra point attempt, however, was foiled when an Ole Miss player hurdled a blocker to tip the kick—an illegal tactic in organized football. Coach Meyer argued his case to no avail.

Disaster! Instead of being tied, Florida was down 31–30. With 3:28 left, the Florida defense needed a quick stop, which it got. Tim had the offense driving, but the Gators faced a fourth-and-one on the Ole Miss 32-yard line. Do you go for a 49-yard field goal to win the game or get the first down and try to get closer?

The Gators were going for it—but the Rebel defense stuffed Tim at the line of scrimmage.

Game over.

When Tim faced the media afterward, he was asked if he wanted to forget the loss. "I don't want to," an emotional Tim replied. "I want it to stay in our hearts and keep hurting so that we'll never let this happen again."

Then he paused and gathered his thoughts. What spilled forth came to be known as "The Promise":

> "I just want to say one thing" . . . *deep breath* . . . "to the fans and everybody in Gator Nation" . . . *pause, sniffle* . . . "I'm sorry. I'm extremely sorry. We were hoping for an undefeated season. That was my goal, something Florida's never done here.
>
> "I promise you one thing: a lot of good will come out of this. You will never see any player in the entire country who will play as hard as I will play the rest of the season. You will never see someone push the rest of the team as hard as I will push everybody the rest of the season.
>
> "You will never see a team play harder than we will the rest of the season. God bless."

With that, Tim exited the post-game podium—and Florida didn't lose another game the rest of the 2008 season.

THREE-SECOND EVANGELISM

Two weeks after the Ole Miss debacle, Tim took the field against LSU suited up like he always was for a home game: blue-jersey-and-white-pants Gator uniform, football pads, cleats, and a helmet. Underneath his eyes, on his upper cheeks, were two black rectangular patches.

Called "eye black," this dark mixture of beeswax, paraffin,

Tim hightailed it to the Broncos' training headquarters in Denver the day after the NFL draft, to hold up his new Broncos jersey and meet the press. (AP Photo/Eric Bakke)

and carbon is applied under the eyes to reduce glare. Sunlight or stadium lights can impair the view of an airborne ball.

Tim began wearing smudges of eye black during Florida day games, but before this important test against the defending national champion LSU Tigers, he had someone in the locker room use a white grease pencil to print **PHL** on top of the black strip underneath his right eye and **4:13** under the left eye. The idea was an out-of-the-box, genuine, clever way to share the biblical message of Philippians 4:13—"I can do all things through Christ who strengthens me"—with millions of football viewers.

Remember, the camera loved Tim Tebow. Throughout the game, TV producers in the truck inserted as many close-up "cutaways" of Tim as they could—like when he was barking out signals in the shotgun or swallowing a spritz of Gatorade on the Florida sideline with his helmet off.

The eye-black-with-a-Bible-verse-story took on a life of its own after the LSU victory, and in every game for the rest of his college career, Tim "shared" a Bible verse with his football-watching audience.

Talk about three-second evangelism. These spiritual billboards sent millions to their Bibles or computers to find out what the verse of the week said. What Tim did with his eye black messages was share his Christian faith, jumpstart a national conversation—and add to his legend.

Tim took some hits from the media, though. "There's something strange about the alliance of modern sports and religion," a columnist with *The Tennessean* opined. Others felt religion and sports should not mix. "Why must he rub it in my face?" was the sentiment of *Orlando Sentinel*'s David Whitley.

None of the potshots fazed Tim or changed the way he played through the rest of the 2008 season. After "The Promise," he actually accomplished what he pledged to do: grab his team by the scruff of the neck and yank them over the national championship goal line with an eight-game winning streak that earned fourth-ranked Florida a date with No. 1-ranked Alabama for the SEC Championship. Alabama was a solid 10-point favorite for this monster match-up in Atlanta.

With star running back Percy Harvin out of the game, an even heavier offensive load fell on Tim's shoulders. The way he took over in the fourth quarter with his team down 20–17, engineering two touchdown drives, ranked right at the top of the Tebow highlight reel. He kept the chains moving by throwing into tight spots and battering the 'Bama defense with muscular runs.

"You knew he was going to lead us to victory," said receiver Carl Moore following a 31–20 triumph that catapulted the Gators into the BCS National Championship Game against top-ranked Oklahoma. "You looked into his eyes, and you could see he was intense. We were all intense."

A HEISMAN REPEAT?

After the Alabama conquest, Tim learned he was again a finalist for the Heisman Trophy—so he and his family repeated the trip to Manhattan. This time at the Nokia Theatre, he was the first to hug Sam Bradford after the Sooner quarterback's name was announced as college football's most outstanding player.

Tim did receive plenty of recognition for his stellar 2008 season—like the Maxwell Award and the Manning Award—but none meant more to him than taking a phone call from Danny Wuerffel, who informed Tim that he'd won the 2008 Wuerffel Trophy, presented annually to the college football player who combines exemplary community service with athletic and academic achievement.

After retiring from professional football in 2004, Danny and his family joined Desire Street Ministries in one of New Orleans' toughest and poorest neighborhoods.

"He's just an amazing young man, an amazing football player," Danny said. "It's funny how things go back and forth. Maybe one day my son will win the Tebow Trophy."

CHAMPIONSHIP GAME MOTIVATION

Florida had one month to prepare for the national championship game, which felt very much like a home game to the Gators since they would be playing the Sam Bradford-led Oklahoma Sooners at Dolphins Stadium in Miami. What made the matchup even more intriguing was that Florida and Oklahoma had *never* played each other before.

Tim didn't have to reach too deep to summon pregame motivation. The acrid smell of the September defeat to Ole Miss still singed his nostrils, and losing the Heisman Trophy vote—despite winning more first-place votes, 309 to 300—certainly smarted.

When Sooners cornerback Dominique Franks popped off that Tim would probably be the fourth-best quarterback in the Big 12 Conference—well, that's all the incentive Tim needed in his wheelhouse.

Properly inspired, Tim decided to forgo **EPH 4:31** and inscribe his eye black with the most widely quoted Bible verse— and one considered the summary of the central doctrine in Christianity—**John 3:16**:

> "For God so loved the world that he gave his one and only Son, that whoever believes in him shall not perish but have eternal life."

Once the BCS championship game started, though, Tim was out of sync. Two interceptions came on balls he shouldn't have thrown. The Oklahoma defense swarmed the line of scrimmage and shut down Tim as well as the Gator ground game. Florida scored only one touchdown in the first half, which would normally put a team in a big hole against a team like Oklahoma, a juggernaut that averaged 50 points a game and rarely had to send their punt team onto the field. But the Gator defense was up to the challenge, and the score was tied 7–7 at halftime.

The Florida defense continued making big stops after intermission, and then Tim got into the flow, converting several big third downs by running and throwing, staking Florida to a small lead. Tim then put a cherry atop the BCS championship sundae when he lobbed a four-yard jump pass to David Nelson with

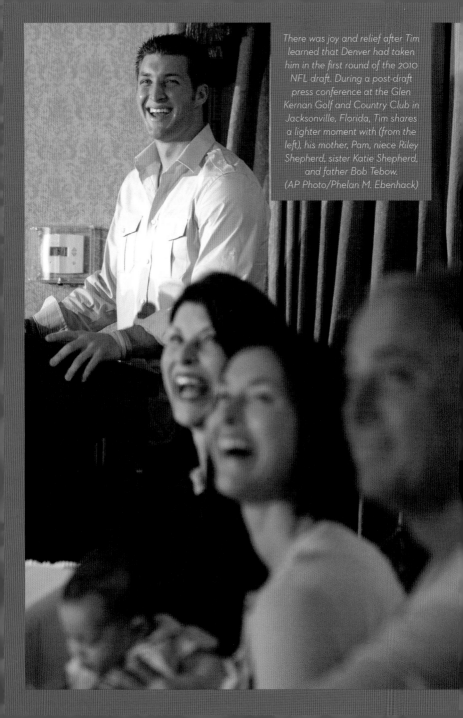

There was joy and relief after Tim learned that Denver had taken him in the first round of the 2010 NFL draft. During a post-draft press conference at the Glen Kernan Golf and Country Club in Jacksonville, Florida, Tim shares a lighter moment with (from the left), his mother, Pam, niece Riley Shepherd, sister Katie Shepherd, and father Bob Tebow. (AP Photo/Phelan M. Ebenhack)

3:07 left in the game, giving Florida a commanding 24–14 lead.

After a four-down stop, all the Florida offense had to do was run out the clock. An exuberant Tim got a bit over-the-top when he celebrated a big 13-yard rush by aiming a "Gator Chomp" at Oklahoma's Nic Harris. Tim fully extended his arms, one above the other, then moved them together and apart to symbolize the opening and closing of an alligator's mouth. An official threw a yellow flag for taunting, and Florida was penalized 15 yards.

"I was pretty excited," Tim said after the game. "Just gave it a little Gator Chomp, and it was also for the fans. I think they kind of enjoyed it." Gator fans also enjoyed how Tim made "The Promise" come true. Everyone on the Florida team believed the Ole Miss loss turned around the season.

Funny how a loss can turn out to be a blessing in more ways than one.

And on a side note, Google reported that searches for "John 3:16" totaled 93 million during and immediately after the BCS victory by Florida.

6
"I'M COMING BACK"

After the national championship-clinching win over Oklahoma, a plaque was affixed to the James W. "Bill" Heavener Football Complex outside The Swamp. Entitled "The Promise," the silver tablet immortalized Tim's emotional post-game speech following the Ole Miss loss.

The idea to mount Tim's heartfelt declaration came from Coach Meyer, who thought Tim's words would inspire future generations of Gators, much the same way Knute Rockne's "Win one for the Gipper" speech back in 1928 had ignited Notre Dame teams over the decades.

Quite an honor—especially for a college football player with one season left to play. Or was Tim bolting to the NFL? He was eligible to turn pro.

"Let's do it again!" he shouted to an estimated 42,000 Gator fans celebrating the team's national championship at The Swamp three days after the victory in Miami. "I'm coming back!"

A few days later, *Sports Illustrated*'s cover showed Tim about to slap his palms in that infamous Gator Chomp against Oklahoma. The headline: NOT DONE YET: TWO TITLES IN THREE YEARS, AND TIM TEBOW IS COMING BACK FOR MORE.

Tim never thought seriously about passing up his senior year to play in the NFL, but he *did* start giving a great deal of thought to what Bible verses he would inscribe on his eye black during his final season in college. Before each game in 2009, Tim lettered a new Bible verse on his eye black, sending millions of fans to their computers to do a Google search.

It turned out Bob Tebow got a preacher after all.

A FAREWELL AT THE SWAMP

For Tim's final home game, against Florida State—Senior Day—Gator fans were urged to wear eye black, with or without an inscribed Bible verse. After Florida whipped its intrastate rival, the Gators had a sparkling 12–0 regular season record, had been ranked No. 1 all season, and were two games away from completing the program's first-ever perfect season.

The stage was set for back-to-back national championships, but first there was some business to conduct against Alabama in the SEC Championship Game, a rematch from the year before held in Atlanta's Georgia Dome.

This time, it was all Crimson Tide. The Florida defense allowed Alabama to convert 11 of 15 third-down opportunities, which kept the Tide rolling down the field and chewing up the game possession clock. Alabama's offense was on the field for 39 minutes, 27 seconds, 20 minutes longer than Florida's.

Instead of giving the Tide a hard-fought game early on, the Gators went meekly into the night, losing 32–13. Their 22-game win streak was toast, the dream of a perfect season rudely ended.

The enduring image from the game is Tim on one knee with his team hopelessly behind as the clock ticks away, tears streaming through his eye black and down his face. He barely held it together during a post-game interview with CBS' sideline reporter, Tracy Wolfson.

"Tim Tearbow" is how some bloggers lit him up, but Tim had one game left in his college career—a January 1 date with No. 5 Cincinnati in the Sugar Bowl.

LOW THROW

If you look at Tim's performance at the 2010 Sugar Bowl, you would think he single-handedly destroyed the Bearcats. He put on a passing exhibition, completing his first 12 passes and going 20-for-23 in the first half for 320 yards and three touchdowns. When it was all over, he had torched Cincinnati for 482 passing yards and supplied the perfect ending to a storied four-year career. The 51–24 annihilation of the previously unbeaten Bearcats left Florida as the only BCS team ever to win at least 13 games in back-to-back seasons.

You'd think Tim would be carried off the field and hailed by the media as one of the greatest college quarterbacks ever. Team Tebow, however, woke up the next day to a media drumbeat that

Tim had private workouts with several NFL teams prior to the 2010 NFL draft, but found a kindred spirit in Josh McDaniels, the boyish-looking 33-year-old head coach of the Broncos. With a passion for football like Tim's, McDaniels wanted the Heisman winner, even if that meant taking him with a first-round pick. (AP Photo/David Zalubowski,File)

started as a whisper but gained concussive force almost overnight: *Tim Tebow is not first-round draft material for the National Football League. In fact, he should consider a position change to tight end.*

In other words, back to the future.

Here's what happened:

With the Sugar Bowl game out of hand, the Fox commentators in the booth, Thom Brennaman and former Baltimore Ravens coach Brian Billick, tossed the topic of Tim's future into the air and batted it around between beer commercials—oops, during lulls in the action.

Does Tim have what it takes to "play at the next level" and become an NFL quarterback?

Cue up the slo-mo of Tim dropping back to pass.

Using a telestrator, Billick dissected Tim's passing motion like a high school biology teacher peeling back the innards of a frog. "You're going to have to change everything he does," the former Ravens coach declared. "He has a windup delivery. He carries the ball too low. And he needs to read his progressions. He's a heck of a player, but how do you make him a first-round pick when you have to change so much?"

Billick's critique certainly made for interesting TV: a former NFL coach slicing up a legendary college player in the midst of the most dominating performance of his career. But what Billick did was bring to light the whispering campaign among NFL general managers and their coaching staffs about Tim's throwing motion—the elongated swoop of his left arm prior to releasing the ball.

The conventional wisdom among NFL cognoscenti was hardening like spackling compound. If Tim wasn't worth a first-round pick in the 2010 NFL draft, was he capable of even playing quarterback at the professional level?

7
PLENTY OF PREDRAFT DRAMA

The instant the 2010 Sugar Bowl game clock struck 00:00, Chase Heavener, who was standing on the floor of the New Orleans Superdome, turned on his Canon 5D Mark II camera—capable of shooting high-quality digital video.

Chase, the son of Bill Heavener (after whom the Heavener Football Complex next to The Swamp is named), was initializing work on a documentary about Tim's road to the NFL. Filming couldn't start until Tim's college career was officially over—to preserve his amateur status—so Chase and his small film crew waited patiently for the final seconds to tick off the Superdome scoreboard. The young filmmaker planned to produce a film about Tim's life from the end of the Sugar Bowl through his first game in the NFL.

It looked like there would be enough drama between the Sugar Bowl and the 2010 NFL draft to fill a miniseries. Tim's opening episode began with the Senior Bowl—a postseason college football exhibition game for graduating seniors played in Mobile, Alabama, in late January. With National Football League coaches and personnel monitoring a week of practices as well as the game, the Senior Bowl would be a showcase for the best prospects in the upcoming NFL draft.

Tim opted to play in the Senior Bowl because he wanted to improve his deteriorating draft standing. Following the Sugar Bowl, NFL scouts were telling reporters—anonymously—that Tim figured to go in the third round and might have to think about playing tight end or H-back, a combination tight end/fullback position. Since Tim wasn't ready to abandon his dream of playing quarterback in the NFL—a yearning of his since he was six years old—he didn't shy away from a week of Senior Bowl practices . . . or from working on his ball placement, footwork, and release.

Team Tebow was aware of the NFL's reservations about his mechanics and loopy throwing motion. In fact, he made the decision to reinvent himself *before* the Senior Bowl by attending the D1 Sports Training facility in Cool Springs, Tennessee, outside Nashville. Tim was one of 18 former college players working out with D1's coaches and trainers.

Tim had visited several other training facilities before deciding on D1, which was co-owned by quarterback Peyton Manning. (Now isn't that ironic?) Waiting for him were several experienced coaches: Marc Trestman, a former quarterbacks coach with Tampa Bay, Cleveland, and Minnesota; Zeke Bratkowski, a longtime NFL coach; former NFL head coach Sam Wyche; and Arizona State University offensive coordinator Noel Mazzone.

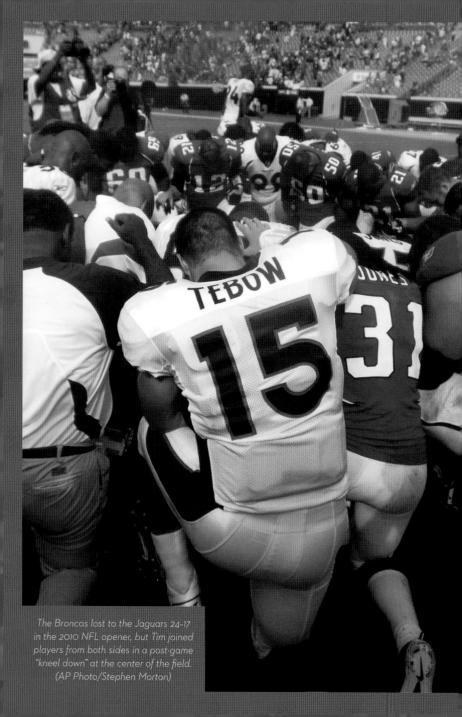

The Broncos lost to the Jaguars 24-17 in the 2010 NFL opener, but Tim joined players from both sides in a post-game "kneel down" at the center of the field. (AP Photo/Stephen Morton)

The D1 coaches worked Tim hard: two hours in the weight room, two hours on the field doing speed work, two hours on quarterback-specific drills, and two hours watching film and studying NFL terminology. Capturing it all was Chase Heavener and his film crew, and the D1 staff downloaded their super slow motion footage into their computers and used the film to show Tim how he could improve his five-step drop, seven-step drop, and throwing motion.

After spending a week in Cool Springs working on his fundamentals, Tim flew to Mobile for the Senior Bowl. He was far from 100 percent: he was battling strep throat, a 103-degree temperature, and a skeptical football media that smelled blood in the water.

When the Senior Bowl was over, Tim can be excused for wishing he'd never played in Mobile. What a dreary late afternoon for No. 15: two fumbles (one lost), four yards rushing on four attempts, and 50 yards passing on 12 attempts, although he did complete eight of his throws. His critics were waiting with long knives.

"It's simple," said one NFL scout. "He's just not a very good quarterback prospect." Scouts Inc. gave Tim a D+ grade, noting that he "put all his weaknesses on display in a setting that did nothing but magnify them." Todd McShay, one of ESPN's NFL draft gurus, was more muted, declaring that Tim "is just not comfortable as a pro-style quarterback."

Only one voice wasn't pessimistic—the one belonging to a feeling-under-the-weather quarterback from Florida. Tim said he improved every day in practice and that his decision to play in the Senior Bowl was proof of his willingness to work hard on his fundamentals. Yet his subpar performance was enough for many NFL coaches and GMs to sell their stock in Tebow, Inc.—despite Tim's 66 percent college career passing percentage, the dozens of passing records he had set in high school and college, and his unworldly 88–16 touchdown-to-interception ratio as a Gator quarterback.

The fact that Tim had been a winner while playing a hybrid style of running back/passing quarterback—where he punished defenses with his left shoulder as well as with his left arm—didn't count for much in the minds of NFL brass or the draft experts.

The Road to a Really Super Sunday

There was another group of film people loitering in New Orleans the night of the Sugar Bowl—this one from Focus on the Family. They were in the Big Easy to discuss the latest developments regarding a 30-second commercial featuring Tim and his mother that would air during the Super Bowl.

Nearly a year earlier, Mark Waters, head of film production at Focus on the Family—a nonprofit Christian organization that offers practical biblical advice on marriage, parenting, and life challenges—had a brainstorm. He envisioned Pam Tebow sharing the story of her son's miraculous birth in an engaging, upbeat way that would be posted as a video on the ministry's website.

Waters pitched the idea to Focus on the Family president Jim Daly, who loved what he heard. *But what about taking the concept a step further? What about involving Tim in the story and turning this into a 30-second commercial for the Super Bowl? Not only would we generate a buzz, but we could impact the culture with a pro-life message rarely heard in the mainstream media.*

Phone calls were made, and a dozen supporters of the Focus on the Family ministry said they would step up and pay the $2.5 million price tag to air a 30-second ad. The next step was to see if the Tebows were on board.

Jim Daly and Ken Windebank, Focus' senior vice president of public affairs, flew to Jacksonville in the fall to float the idea past Bob and Pam. The Tebows signaled their interest and said they were open to the concept. They were grateful that this 30-second film would be viewed by millions watching the Super Bowl.

On Tuesday, January 12, 2010, everyone met at a soundstage at Full Sail Studios in Winter Park, Florida, just outside Orlando. Pam and Tim looked natural as they spoke their lines in front of a white seamless background.

When the filming was completed, Focus on the Family announced in a January 15 press release that the Tebows had decided to participate in a Super Bowl ad "because the issue of life is one they feel strongly about." CBS—the broadcasting network for the upcoming February 7 Super Bowl—had approved the advertisement based on the test commercial.

With that benign statement, the Tebows tipped over a hornet's nest. Hearing the howls of protest by women's groups in favor of "choice" and "reproductive freedom," you would have thought the end of Western civilization was imminent. The National Organization of Women (NOW), the Feminist Majority, and Women's Media Center called on CBS to scrap the Tebow Super Bowl ad because it was likely to convey an anti-abortion message. NOW labeled the ad "extraordinarily offensive and demeaning."

No one, of course, had viewed the ad, which wouldn't be shown until Super Sunday.

With the benefit of hindsight, which is always 20/20, the outrage over the Tebows' Super Bowl ad seems rather silly now.

Like a brilliant fake in the open field, the Tebow ad left detractors flummoxed, flat-footed, and gasping for air. The national reaction, especially from a mainstream media that usually takes the pro-choice side, could be summed up in one sentence: *What was all the fuss about?*

The Focus ad ran in the first quarter and started with Pam, dressed in a simple black outfit, standing against a white background. Above pleasing guitar chords, she spoke in an appealing, warm manner—like she entered your living room with a cup of primrose tea in her hand.

> **Pam:** I call him my miracle baby. He almost didn't make it into this world. I can remember so many times when I almost lost him. It was so hard. Well, he's all grown up now, and I still worry about his health. You know, with all our family's been through, you have to be tough.

> *Suddenly Tim plows in from stage left and tackles his mom to the floor. But she pops up, hair barely mussed, and addresses her son with a coy scold in her voice:*

Tim's first game as a professional was staged in his backyard—Jacksonville, Florida. The early September game was played in muggy heat and offered little to cheer about for the thousands of Tebow fans. Tim was on the field for three plays—including this one-yard burst before a welcome-to-the-NFL hit by former University of Florida teammate Derrick Harvey. (AP Photo/Eric Bakke)

Pam: Timmy! I'm trying to tell our story here.

Tim: Sorry about that, Mom. You still worry about me, Mom?

Pam: Well, yeah. You're not nearly as tough as I am.

"No mention of abortion, no recounting of the dramatic story," wrote *Politics Daily* columnist David Gibson. "No need. Without any frame of reference, the spot could have been a pitch for osteoporosis medication or the need for universal health care or a reminder not to forget Mother's Day. But everyone knew what the ad was about and the ad didn't have to say anything directly, which is the definition of the perfect advocacy ad. It was charming and disarming and went with the flow of the Super Bowl mania."

Jim Daly said afterward that the CBS network would not permit the word *abortion* to be mentioned anyway, but who knows how many reconsidered their view of abortion?

8
COMBINE TIME

Tim returned to Cool Springs, still working to get rid of his swooping windup to pass the ball more quickly.

Was he overhauling his throwing motion? Not really, he said.

"It's more of a tweak," Tim told the press. "It's not necessarily changing my whole motion, just the way I'm holding the ball and kind of how I'm getting to where I'm throwing it. That's kind of the biggest problem we've seen, so that's what we're working on the most."

Tim practiced over and over holding the football higher—at shoulder height—after he received the snap. That movement effectively cut the loop from his throwing motion.

B-roll from Chase Heavener's film crew released to ESPN and other media outlets showing Tim—under the gaze of his D1 coaches—dropping back seven steps with his left arm cocked high before delivering a tightly thrown pass. Even casual fans could tell his throwing motion was more compact and that he was "getting" to his releases quicker.

Between working on this throwing motion and hopping on private planes to make appearances at the Super Bowl, the Daytona 500, and the National Prayer Breakfast in Washington, D.C., Tim worked insanely hard during the month of February.

Kurt Hester, the corporate director of training at D1, said Tim's work ethic was a problem—"he just goes all-out all the time." Working around all the out-of-state appearances had been tough, Hester said, "but he won't quit. If I told him to get here at three in the morning, he'd get here at three in the morning."

Coming up during the first week of March was the National Invitational Camp, otherwise known as the NFL Combine, which is named after three scouting camps that "combined" or merged in 1985. More than 600 NFL personnel, including head coaches, general managers, and scouts, converged on Indianapolis for the camp.

The 329 players who expected to be drafted were invited to Lucas Oil Field to be weighed and measured and to participate in six measurable drills—40-yard dash, 225-pound bench press repetitions, vertical jump, broad jump, three-cone drill, and shuttle run—as well as individual drills. There would also be psychological evaluations and an IQ exam known as the Wonderlic Test.

The process can be dehumanizing; some call the NFL Combine the "Underwear Olympics" and compare the physicals to being poked and prodded like steers on a hoof. The extensive medical exams, which could last up to eight hours, had players clad only in undershorts, standing in a room full of NFL team doctors and scouts as they were weighed, measured, and subjected to a battery of tests—MRIs, EKGs, CT scans, X-rays, and more.

Aspiring NFL players dare not skip the Combine, and Tim flew to Indianapolis to participate, even though he said he would not participate in individual throwing drills. Tim said he would instead wait until the pro day at his alma mater to put his arm to the test in front of NFL evaluators.

Pro days are held at each university under conditions thought to be more favorable for the players. At their pro days, quarterbacks participate in passing drills, and position players run the 40-yard dash, make a vertical jump, do the three-cone drill, and undergo other physical tests in front of an array of NFL coaches and scouts.

The NFL Combine—an entirely different bird—is a four-day process that begins with a preliminary medical examination and orientation. During his first night in Indianapolis Tim went through a process called "speed dating"—where representatives of every NFL team sit at tables inside small rooms and conduct 10-to-15-minute interviews with each of the players.

If a prospect isn't in good shape physically, the NFL has a way of finding out. The second day is reserved for four extensive medical exams—eight doctors at a time, one from each of the 32 NFL teams. If players, especially quarterbacks, had fudged on their height and weight, it was now out in the open.

Here's how Tim Tebow measured up: 6-2¾, 236 pounds.

Since his college career ended, Tim has worked on his mechanics and throwing motion. Critics felt he had too much of a wind-up and needed to tighten his delivery. (AP Photo/ Derek Gee)

Tim was usually listed at 6-3, so he wasn't too far off the mark.

For quarterbacks, the 40-yard dash ranks far down on the list of priorities; height, arm strength, quick release, escapability, leadership skills, and football knowledge are what matter to the NFL. Ditto for the standing broad jump, a drill where former Texas QB Colt McCoy excelled, vaulting nine feet, six inches, but Tim just beat him out, clearing nine feet, seven inches. Tim also wowed the scouts with his 38.5-inch vertical leap, which tied him for the Combine's all-time record for quarterbacks, held by Josh McCown. By way of comparison, Tim's leap was a half-inch higher than Michael Vick's in 2001. He completed five of the six measurable drills, passing on the 225-pound bench press repetitions so he could protect his throwing arm.

There was one individual drill Tim performed at the NFL Combine, however, where you could say his time was a revelation: in the three-cone drill, Tim ran a hell-blazing 6.66 seconds, which showed he was a real speed demon.

PRO DAYS AHEAD

With so much at stake—draft position, which team would pick them, and millions of dollars—quarterbacks aspiring to an NFL career leave little to chance. Very few throw at the NFL Combine because they will be passing to unfamiliar receivers at an unfamiliar venue. NFL coaches can also dictate which passing drills they would like to see at the Combine.

As they say at golf's biggest tournaments, you can't win a major on the first day, but you sure can lose it with a poor outing.

Tim was into his second month of working to get rid of his below-the-belt throwing motion and to perfect the above-the-shoulder delivery NFL coaches like to see in their quarterbacks. The more time he had to practice and improve his new technique, the better chance he had to impress coaches and scouts when it came time to throw at his pro day.

Tim was first to fire up for pro day, and as you would expect, the March 17 event at the University of Florida was a circus. "For all the television time, Internet bandwidth, and newsprint used to discuss Tim Tebow's new throwing motion, anything short of the southpaw walking onto Florida Field and throwing right-handed was found to be a bitter disappointment," wrote *Sports Illustrated*'s Andy Staples.

More than 3,000 spectators and 100 NFL personnel were on hand at The Swamp, including five head coaches and a couple of general managers. Tim wasn't the only Gator athlete under the microscope; teammates Carlos Dunlap, Joe Haden, Aaron Hernandez, and Maurkice Pouncey—all potential first-rounders—were going through their pro day paces as well.

Tim threw for 45 minutes—outs, curls, hitches, posts, comebacks, and gos. He cocked the ball closer to his ear, released the ball much more quickly, and delivered tight spirals where they needed to be. He hit receiver David Nelson on a 45-yard post pattern—in stride. Next throw, the same 45-yard post but to the opposite side of the field, where the deep pass landed in Riley Cooper's arms in full gait.

Tim looked flat-out impressive. The backpedaling on his

seven-step drops was an athletic work of art, his command of the field was sure, and his passing was on the money. The debut of his new throwing motion went off without a hitch.

Like the opening of a hit show on Broadway, Tim's new act drew raves. The consensus in the media was that he had shown "ridiculous" improvement. In less than an hour on his favorite field, Tim successfully pushed back a tide of coaching opinion that had threatened to sink his chances of ever playing quarterback in the NFL. He was once again a viable NFL quarterback prospect.

Between pro day and NFL draft day five weeks later, Tim scheduled private workouts with several NFL teams, including Seattle, Washington, and New England.

Tim also hoped to get a closer look from the Denver Broncos. During one of the "speed dates" at the NFL Combine, he had sat in a meeting room just a few feet apart from Josh McDaniels, the boyish-looking 33-year-old head coach of the Broncos. They were talking football, and the energy level rose as their eyes locked and their ideas spilled forth. In a word, they *clicked.*

The 15 minutes passed by way too quickly. Tim felt jacked as he left the room. He had met someone with the same passion for football that he had himself. Coach McDaniels was just as intense, just as juiced about finding a way to win in the NFL. He understood where Tim was coming from.

Tim stood up and shook hands with the Broncos coach and left the meeting not wanting to visit with another team.

9
THE 2010 NFL DRAFT

It used to be that character didn't count for much in the National Football League.

As long as you could deliver blistering hits in the open field, create a hole in the line, make a catch in traffic, or run the two-minute offense, you pretty much got a free pass.

Back in the day, fans were amused by the antics of Broadway Joe Namath—he of the white llama rugs and "bachelor pad" fame who titled a chapter in his 1970 autobiography "I Like My Girls Blonde and My Johnny Walker Red."

Those relatively innocent days are as long gone as love beads and incense sticks.

Between January 2000 and the spring of 2010, arrests, citations, and drunk-driving charges involving NFL players piled up—495 according to an investigative article in the *San Diego Union-Tribune*. It seems like there's a report every week about an

In the January 2012 playoff game in Denver, Tim is about to take a hit from a Pittsburgh Steelers lineman in early action. In leading the Broncos to an overtime victory, Tim passed for 316 yards, completing ten throws for an average of 31.6 yards per completion. A coincidence? John 3:16 was the most popular Google search the following Monday. (AP Photo/G. Newman Lowrance)

NFL player arrested for public intoxication, driving under the influence, brandishing a weapon, battering a girlfriend, getting caught in a bar fight, or being charged with sexual assault.

One of the most scandalous affairs was an alleged sex party early in the 2005 season involving hookers and 17 Minnesota Viking football players—including the team's starting quarterback—aboard a pair of chartered boats on Lake Minnetonka.

For years, some NFL teams have closed one eye to character issues in their evaluation of draft prospects. The St. Louis Rams drafted running back Lawrence Phillips in 1996 despite the fact that he received a six-game suspension during his senior year at the University of Nebraska for dragging his girlfriend by her hair down a flight of stairs. The Rams believed the on-the-field reward of playing Phillips in the backfield outweighed any off-the-field risk. Bad call. Phillips was arrested three times in two seasons before the Rams released him . . . for insubordination.

When quarterbacks Peyton Manning and Ryan Leaf were in the running to be selected first in the 1998 NFL draft, Indianapolis Colts president Bill Polian made appointments to meet with both at the NFL Combine. Manning showed up on time, groomed and mature, while Leaf blew off the appointment.

Small actions make big impressions, and the Colts took Manning as the No. 1 pick and were richly rewarded. The Chargers followed with Ryan Leaf, who quickly unimpressed his teammates and coaches with a lousy work ethic, surly attitude, and profane outbursts at members of the media. Leaf was one of the more remarkable flameouts in NFL history, and many point to his character, or lack of it, as the main reason why.

Then came a disturbing period between April 2006 and April 2007, when the NFL realized it had a serious problem with players of poor conduct and character. At least 79 incidents, including a series of high-profile arrests involving Tennessee Titans cornerback Adam "Pacman" Jones and Cincinnati Bengals wide receiver Chris Henry, prompted Commissioner Roger Goodell to decree a tough personal conduct policy.

When it seemed like NFL rookies stood a better chance of making the police blotter than the team that drafted them, Goodell and the league had to look at a different way of doing things. The commissioner's personal conduct policy spurred NFL front office personnel to rethink the criteria they used when considering a professional football player.

"CHARACTER GUYS"

In recent years, the buzzword in NFL draft war rooms—thank goodness—has been *character*. These days, you're apt to hear GMs say, "He's a character guy," for someone on their draft board, or "He had character issues" for a player they passed on.

Character is one of those intangibles that may be hard to define but is easy to recognize. As someone once pointed out, character means having the inward motivation to do what's right even when nobody is looking. Character means practicing self-restraint regardless of the circumstances. In light of that, it might be a good idea for every football player to memorize this observation from nineteenth-century American newspaper editor Horace

Greeley: "Fame is a vapor, popularity an accident, riches take wing, but only character endures."

Going into the 2010 NFL draft, coaches and team personnel were paying attention to character more than ever in making their player evaluations. That's part of why many teams thought so highly of Sam Bradford, Colt McCoy, and Tim Tebow, who were all outspoken about their faith. While there were internal debates about Sam's right shoulder, Colt's height, or Tim's throwing motion, there was a league-wide consensus that these three quarterbacks were "character guys"—upstanding young men with a strong moral compass.

When the 2010 NFL draft arrived, it turned out that character played a huge role for Sam, Colt, and Tim. Their attitude, work ethic, disposition, and respect for authority were the determining factors in where the Three QBs landed during the draft. Bradford went number one overall to the St. Louis Rams. McCoy, not expected to be a first rounder, went to the Cleveland Browns with the 85th pick.

And then there was Tebow. . .

TIM TEBOW: THE FIRST-ROUND SHOCKER

Tim Tebow was in New York City, too, but not for the NFL draft. He had traveled to Manhattan a couple days earlier to promote *NCAA Football 11*, EA Sports' new college football video game. After making an appearance at an upscale restaurant on lower Broadway and playing his brother Robby in the football video game—Tim was Virginia Tech and Robby was Florida—

Tim announced he would fly back to Jacksonville to accompany his family for the draft, even though he was one of 18 players the NFL had invited to attend.

"It would have been exciting to be here, to hold your jersey up with the commissioner. That's always something every athlete wants to do," Tim told NFL Network's Charles Davis the day before the draft. "But it's going to be special being at home. Being with my family, my friends, my best friends, my high school teammates, people like that that I know couldn't make their way up here, that I wanted to be able to spend this moment with. That's what it's truly about for me."

The prospect of sitting in the Radio City Music Hall green room—with TV cameras recording every nose twitch until his name was called—understandably lacked appeal in the Tebow camp. Who wants to squirm on national TV as the pressure mounts when you're passed over?

Tim and his parents had no idea whether Tim would be picked in the first round or drop ingloriously to the second, third, or—gasp!—fourth. From the going-out-on-top Sugar Bowl victory to the Senior Bowl washout to the raves he received for his revamped throwing motion at pro day, Tim's stock among NFL teams fluctuated like the Dow Jones average.

Throughout the spring of 2010, one of the biggest stories in sports remained: *Where will Tim Tebow be drafted?* If an NFL player or coach wanted to get some face time with the media, all he had to do was venture an opinion on Tim's draft day prospects.

Tim is one of the most intense athletes on the planet, whose will to win is matched by few others. In this shot from the playoff game against Pittsburgh in early 2012, Tim was fired up after scoring a second-quarter touchdown. (AP Photo/Jack Dempsey)

Tim's former teammate at Florida, Cincinnati Bengals wide receiver Andre Caldwell, said the right spot to draft the Gator quarterback would be "late second round," adding that the former Heisman winner would need significant time to adjust to life in the NFL. Following Tim's pro day, Miami Dolphins quarterback Chad Henne bluntly told WQAM radio in Miami, "My judgment is that he's not an NFL quarterback. I'll leave it at that."

That's precisely what draftnik Mel Kiper Jr. had been saying since the end of Tim's junior year, when he began ringing the town bell, proclaiming that Tim wasn't NFL quarterback material—and would be better suited to playing professional football as a tight end or H-back. The helmet-haired analyst dissed everything about Tim's quarterbacking skills.

To his credit, Tim did an interview on ESPN Radio with host Freddie Coleman and Kiper at the end of his junior season. The Florida quarterback showed he could think on his feet just as quickly as he could move them after a snap count. "You tell me this," Tim said during his radio exchange with Kiper. "What do you think I need to do to be an NFL quarterback? You tell me that."

Kiper backpedaled like an All-Pro cornerback and mumbled something about the NFL being a "flip of the coin" and that Peyton Manning had his detractors when he came into the league. Said Kiper, "You're too good with the ball in your hands not to think, *Could he be Frank Wycheck? Could he be Chris Cooley?* That's why," Kiper said. "You're too good, doing what you do,

Tim, running with the football."

Wycheck and Cooley were NFL tight ends, but in this context, the comment was a thinly veiled insult since Tim's peers were quarterbacks like Sam Bradford and Colt McCoy, not journeymen tight ends.

After hearing Kiper out, the Florida quarterback replied, "The quarterback has the ball in his hands every play."

Touché, Tim . . .

In the weeks leading up to the 2010 NFL draft, Tim's name was nowhere to be found on Kiper's "Big Board" of Top 25 picks, but "he's the story of the draft, like him or not," said Peter King of *Sports Illustrated*. For every Tebow doubter, though, there was a Tebow booster. Perhaps the biggest voice in his corner was former Tampa Bay coach Jon Gruden, who had worked out Tim as part of *Gruden's QB Camp* specials that ran on ESPN leading up to draft day. Gruden told anyone who would listen that Tim could very well crack the first round.

"If you want Tim to be on your football team, if you want him bad enough, you're going to have him in the first round or the second," Gruden said. "If you want Tim in your locker room, on your football team, and you can see a little down the road, a team like that is going to take him earlier than some people expect. I'm very confident in this guy."

Preceding the draft, five NFL teams requested private individual workouts with Tim, including the Denver Broncos, whose young head coach, Josh McDaniels, was said to be intrigued with Tim—even though the club had recently traded for Cleveland's

Brady Quinn, a third-year pro out of Notre Dame. In the week preceding the draft, the Broncos visited and worked out Tim twice in a five-day span.

Kiper and his ESPN sidekick, Todd McShay, stuck to their guns regarding Tim's draft prospects. "I think Tim has got to develop into a starting quarterback to be worth being a second-round choice," said Kiper, showing his belief that the first round was beyond the realm of reason for Tebow. "I don't think he can be. Others do. We'll see . . . I'll root for Tim to prove me wrong on that one."

McShay called Tim a "project" and said he'd be surprised if any team parted with a cherished first-round pick for him. "I would not draft Tebow in the first two rounds. My philosophy is you draft people who have a legitimate shot to be a starter right away."

Through it all, Tim's faith and confidence never wavered. On the morning of the NFL draft, he told *USA Today*, "I believe I'll be drafted as a quarterback and used as a quarterback."

Tim watched the draft unfold at a private residence at Jacksonville's Glen Kernan Country Club, surrounded by two or three dozen family members, close friends, and others in the Tebow camp, including his agent, Jimmy Sexton. Sitting in the corner of the living room was a cardboard box stuffed with Denver Broncos hats.

They knew.

But you need a flow chart to follow the Broncos' crazy route to using the No. 25 pick to select Tim Tebow.

- First, the Broncos traded their No. 11 pick to the San Francisco 49ers for the Niners' first-round pick (No. 13) and a fourth-round pick.

- Next, the Broncos sent the No. 13 pick to Philadelphia in exchange for the Eagles' first-round pick (No. 24) and two third-rounders.

- Then the Broncos traded the No. 24 pick (as well as a fourth-round choice) to New England for the Patriots' first-round pick (No. 22), which they used *not* to draft Tim Tebow but Georgia Tech receiver Demaryius Thomas. (Keep track of this name.)

- Three picks later, the Broncos grabbed the No. 25 pick from Baltimore in exchange for Denver's second-, third-, and fourth-round picks. The Broncos also received the No. 119 pick in the deal.

All this shuffling momentarily confused the ESPN talking heads. Could it be that Denver . . . ?

And that's when Tim's cell phone rang with a 303 area code. "Should I answer it?" he asked his agent, Jimmy Sexton.

Of course, Tim.

Coach McDaniels was on the line, but he didn't seem at all in a hurry to get down to business. He made small talk and asked Tim if he was enjoying the night. *Oh, and by the way, we're going to trade up and take you.*

The electrifying news swept through the living room just as an ESPN camera cut away to the joyful scene of Tim hugging his

The originator of "tebowing" practices what he quietly preaches, taking a knee before the start of the Broncos' home game against Chicago, December 11, 2011. (AP Photo/Joe Mahoney)

family and friends. Then Team Tebow brought out the Broncos hats, and Tim, wearing an ear-to-ear grin, slipped one on.

At 10:09 p.m., in the midst of the pandemonium, Commissioner Goodell's official announcement came that Tim Tebow was a first-round draft choice of the Denver Broncos.

The proclamation sent shock waves through Radio City Music Hall and caused Mel Kiper Jr. to blanche like he'd just swallowed a dose of cod liver oil.

"I just think I showed them [the Broncos] I was willing to do whatever it took," Tim told ESPN. "I want to thank everyone in the organization. Over the last few weeks, we really hit it off. I was hoping and praying that was where I could play."

Tim said his private workout three days earlier with the Denver coaching staff raised his hopes that Denver would be the team that would take him. "It was awesome," he said of his day in Denver. "It was a day full of ball. We talked ball, watched film. We watched so much stuff . . . . It was the best day I've had. I enjoyed it. Their coaches are awesome. It was great. Their coaches are just like the coaches I have at Florida. I'm just excited to be a Bronco."

The Denver media reported that the Broncos knocked the NFL on its insignia ears by selecting Tim, and headlines around the country called Denver's drafting of Tim "surprising" and "shocking."

There was electricity in the rarefied Colorado air, but there were also some interesting dynamics regarding the pick. The Centennial State is really the tale of two cities: Denver, the state capital, and

Colorado Springs, 60 miles to the south, along the Front Range corridor. Denver (and nearby Boulder) is uniformly more liberal, while Colorado Springs, which is home to dozens of Christian ministries, including Focus on the Family, is more conservative.

Would Tim be a polarizing figure in such an environment?

"Tim Tebow is a lightning rod," said Bill McCartney, the former University of Colorado football coach and founder of the Promise Keepers men's ministry. But, he added, "There is an anointing on Tim and his family. He's one of those guys who comes along who has God's handprints all over him." McCartney predicted that Tim, who's heavily involved in philanthropic efforts through his Tim Tebow Foundation, would make a difference for Denver's poor and oppressed.

Perhaps that's why *Denver Post* columnist Woody Paige—a regular panelist on the ESPN sports-talk program *Around the Horn* who is not known for any conservative views—preached tolerance shortly after Tim was drafted. The headline on his sympathetic column: IT'S NOT FAIR TO RIP TEBOW FOR HIS FAITH.

Maybe the Mile High City took Paige's column to heart. It was about to start on an improbable journey with Tim Tebow—and declare its love.

10
ROOKIE YEAR

Being an NFL rookie quarterback is a tough gig.

From their first snap, first-year signal callers discover that the pro game is played at a much faster pace than in college. They are pitted against more athletic defenses, and they must perform under a new spotlight. Because NFL players are paid for their services, home-field fans feel freer to vent their displeasure after an interception or a three-and-out series. The local media, often friendly boosters in college towns, delight in carving up pro players like a Thanksgiving turkey—proving the adage that the pen is mightier than the sword.

It generally takes a few seasons for a young quarterback to mature and feel comfortable in the National Football League. That's why Drew Brees caddied for Doug Flutie during his rookie year with the San Diego Chargers in 2001, playing in just one game. When Philip Rivers was drafted behind Brees in 2004, he threw only three passes as a third-string rookie.

Those who *do* play a lot during their first season in the pros take their lumps while adapting to a faster and tougher professional game. For nearly every hotshot collegian entering the league, it's *normal* to struggle in the rookie season. Learning an NFL offense is like learning a new language, and with speedy 250-pound linebackers shooting through the gaps, it's easy to see why rookie quarterbacks are often overwhelmed when they line up behind center.

Looking at today's ranks of premier quarterbacks, only one held his own in his first year of pro ball:

- **Peyton Manning,** playing with the Indianapolis Colts, set five different NFL rookie records, including most touchdown passes in a season, but he also threw a league-high 28 interceptions for a team that struggled to a 3–13 record.
- **Tom Brady**, drafted almost as an afterthought by the New England Patriots in the sixth round, started the 2000 season as the fourth-string quarterback. He threw just three passes his rookie year, completing one.
- **Michael Vick**, the No. 1 draft choice in 2001, was brought along slowly by Atlanta Falcons head coach Dan Reeves. He played in eight games, starting two, while experiencing marginal success for a team that finished 7–9.

Six weeks into the 2010 season, against the New York Jets at Invesco Field, Tim saw his greatest action to date—rushing six times, including a five-yard touchdown run. Always a demonstrative player, Tim leaps into the arms of his teammate Dan Gronkowski, a tight end.
(AP Photo/ Bill Nichols)

- **Aaron Rodgers** arrived in Green Bay in 2005 where Brett Favre was only in his 15th season. Rodgers saw limited action in three games.
- **Ben Roethlisberger**, thrust into a starting role early due to injuries, turned in the best season ever for a rookie QB in 2004, going 13–0 as a starter and leading the Pittsburgh Steelers to the AFC Championship game.

Tim arrived in Denver supremely happy that he'd been picked in the first round by the Broncos. The local media swooned over the Florida quarterback, even admitting they were seduced by his charismatic charm and his aw-shucks, Jack Armstrong, all-American attitude. Many fans warmed to the idea that Tim could take hold of the franchise like Hall of Famer John Elway did in the 1980s and 1990s.

If Tim had worked hard in the months leading up the NFL draft, he doubled down during training camp. Tim told reporters he had a saying on his bedroom wall at home: "Hard work beats talent when talent doesn't work hard."

His presence drew a record 3,100 fans to the first day of training camp, and Tim worked his way past Brady Quinn on the depth chart to establish himself as the No. 2 quarterback behind starter Kyle Orton. In the middle of summer camp, Tim showed that he wasn't a prima donna by readily submitting to a ridiculous "Friar Tuck" haircut—a humongous bald spot on top of his dome surrounded by a ring of hair. Looking like he stepped out of a Robin Hood and Sheriff of Nottingham movie, the monk haircut was part of a rookie hazing ceremony. Tim said he went along with the gag to build team chemistry.

For most of the 2010 season, as the team kept losing and losing, the Broncos' team chemistry wasn't good. Sure, head coach Josh McDaniels—who made it no secret that Tim was his pet project—featured him in the team's "Wild Horse" packages on third-and-short and goal-line situations early in the season, but Tim was kept on the shortest leash possible. He didn't throw his first pass until the middle of the November—a mini three-yard touchdown toss.

By then, the Bronco season was already in tatters, but the worst was yet to come. During the last week of October, the Broncos had flown to London, England, to play the San Francisco 49ers as part of the NFL's "International Series" outreach. Steve Scarnecchia, the team's director of video operations, taped the 49ers' walkthrough practice at Wembley Stadium—and was caught doing so. The practice is strictly forbidden.

The media dubbed it "Spygate II" because what transpired was reminiscent of the New England Patriots' Spygate scandal of 2007–08. Since McDaniels was a Patriots assistant coach at the time and a Bill Belichick acolyte . . . well, you can connect the dots.

McDaniels was fired in early December for his role in Spygate II as well as the Broncos' 3–9 belly flop. With the disastrous season going nowhere and starting quarterback Kyle Orton out with injured ribs, diehard Broncos fans—and the Denver media—clamored for something to cheer about. *Give Tebow the rock!*

With three games left on the schedule, interim head coach Eric Studesville decided it really was Tebow Time, naming Tim the starter for a road game against the Oakland Raiders.

With Silver and Black fans screaming "Tebow Bust! Tebow Bust!", Tim electrified his teammates by galloping up the gut for a 40-yard touchdown—and endeared himself to his fans when he admitted afterward that he was supposed to hand the ball to running back Correll Buckhalter. In other words, he scored on a busted play.

Although Denver lost to Oakland, Tim infused energy into the Broncos players, showing leadership and determination. He also had the dirtiest Denver uniform when the clock ran out.

The following game, against the Houston Texans, became the first installment of the Tebow legend in Denver. Playing before a boisterous sellout crowd with only 5,717 no-shows, the Broncos fell behind 17–0 at halftime—which was par for their season. A Tebow interception in the end zone didn't help their cause.

Then, after intermission, something special happened. Tim unleashed a 50-yard bomb to receiver Jabar Gaffney on the opening drive of the second half that led to a touchdown. The next two drives resulted in a field goal and another touchdown. With the Bronco defense suddenly developing a spine, Denver was down just 23–17 with 7:42 remaining.

A clutch third-and-10 dump-off pass netted 22 yards. Then Tim lasered a 15-yard strike, followed by an 11-yard scramble. Down at the 6 yard line, Tim took the ball in the shotgun, shook off a sack, and had the football sense to pivot to his left where there was plenty of green grass and no white Houston uniforms in the vicinity. Tim won the footrace to the pylon, and Denver's comeback was complete, 24–23.

If you can't chuck it, then tuck it.

Bronco supporters rejoiced that their team had snapped a five-game losing streak, and some fans believed a star was born that afternoon against Houston. Speculation ran rampant about whether Tim was a modern-day Moses who would lead the Broncos out of the wilderness and into the Promised Land of the NFL playoffs.

Tim's three-game audition probably raised as many questions as answers about his future as an NFL quarterback. He certainly proved that he belonged behind center and could lead his team down the field, seemingly by force of will. But being an NFL quarterback was a lot more than a seven-step drop and flinging the ball down the field, as Tim was learning.

Bronco legend John Elway, who was named executive vice president of football operations following the disastrous 2010 season, said Tim needed to work on the fundamentals of being a pocket passer and anticipating throws. "We all agree on one thing," Elway said. "Tim Tebow is a darn good football player. What we have to make him is a darn good quarterback, and that is what we have to figure out."

TELLING HIS STORY

On May 31, 2011, I (Mike Yorkey) flew with my wife, Nicole, to her native county of Switzerland. Our routing that day took

us from San Diego to Washington, D.C.'s Dulles Airport to Geneva. We were traveling to attend the wedding of Nicole's goddaughter, Seraina.

I was on a mission as soon as I stepped off the plane in Washington—find a copy of *Through My Eyes,* Tim's autobiography written with collaborator Nathan Whitaker. May 31 was the day the book went on sale. Hey, I didn't mind paying full freight in the airport bookstore because *Through My Eyes* was an enjoyable read that made the hours pass quickly as our red-eye flight crossed the Atlantic. I would have liked a little less football and a little more personal stuff—like why sexual purity was important to him—but *Through My Eyes* was a fine, worthwhile book.

The public agreed with me. *Through My Eyes* became the No. 1 bestselling Christian book in 2011, with around 400,000 copies sold. With the NFL lockout in full swing, Tim had time to make the promotional rounds in New York, giving numerous print and TV interviews. The 23-year-old QB quipped, "Most people wait until they're at least 24 to put out an autobiography." Tim also participated in massive book signings in his home state of Florida, where long lines formed hours before his arrival. He cheerfully signed hundreds of books in two-hour appearances—which had to put some stress on his throwing arm.

Meanwhile, pro football fans everywhere were stressed about whether there would even be a 2011 season. Tim was not allowed any contact with his coaches or to step on the grounds of the Bronco training facility in Denver, where he could have met with new head coach John Fox, worked on his mechanics, and learned coverages during the off-season.

When the lockout finally ended and the players got into training camp, it soon became evident there was a new pecking order on the depth chart: Tim had lost his starting quarterback position to Kyle Orton and was fighting Brady Quinn for the backup job. There were even rumors that the Broncos were going to wash their hands of Tim by releasing him.

Taking note of the situation, ESPN columnist Rick Reilly wrote that Tim was a "nice kid, sincere as a first kiss, but he's not ready yet, might never be ready. Somebody alert the Filipino missionaries. If he doesn't improve, he might be among them sooner than we thought."

Tim kept plugging away and working hard, but it was hard to gain experience when he was getting crumbs—a few fourth-quarter snaps in preseason games against the other team's third string. When the season started, Orton was firmly entrenched as the starter.

The Broncos split their first two games at home, losing to Oakland but bouncing back to beat the playoff-bound Cincinnati Bengals. A close road loss to the Tennessee Titans and a blowout by the Green Bay Packers had the natives getting restless. Employees at Multiline International Imports, which has a large digital sign adjoining Interstate 25, the main north-south corridor in Denver, decided to express their frustration with the team's tailspin by printing the following message on their billboard:

BRONCOS FANS TO JOHN FOX: PLAY TEBOW!

Talk about a quarterback controversy. Denver fans chanted "Tebow! Tebow!" after each three-and-out by the inept offense, and the pressure intensified on Coach Fox to yank Orton and give Tim a chance. The boo birds were really giving it to the coaching staff when the Broncos fell behind 23–10 against the San Diego Chargers in Denver. Those catcalls turned to cheers, however, when Coach Fox benched Orton in favor of Tim in the second half. After a scoreless third quarter, the Broncos were way behind, 26–10, but then the fourth-quarter magic started: Tim scrambling for a 12-yard touchdown . . . Tim throwing a 28-yard touchdown pass . . . Tim driving his team in the last minute. Only a batted-down "Hail Mary" pass in the end zone preserved the Chargers' 29–24 victory.

"He makes plays, you can't deny that," said relieved Chargers' linebacker, Takeo Spikes. "People can talk about the way he throws the ball, people can talk about his release. But at the end of the day, this league is about *What have you done for me lately?* And if you can come in and make plays that another can't, then you'll play a long time."

The Broncos were now 1–4. Coach Fox noticed the spark in his players when Tim was under center. Should he dump Orton and turn the team over to Tebow? Their next game was in Miami against the Dolphins.

With a bye week coming up, he had some time to think about it.

THE MIRACLE IN MIAMI

NFL teams aren't supposed to win games in which they've been shut out for 55 minutes and struggled to put together a first down, let alone a decent drive. The Broncos were down 15–0 in Miami, and Tim was either overthrowing or short-hopping his frustrated receivers. If he had been a baseball pitcher, he was throw-it-to-the-backstop wild.

The Dolphins, thinking they had the game well in hand, put their defense in "prevent" mode with 5:23 left. Denver was eating up time when, out of nowhere, Tim hit Matt Willis on a crossing pattern for a 42-yard gain that took the Broncos down to the 12-yard line. Three plays later, Tim found Demaryius Thomas in the corner of the end zone. Now the score was 15–7, with only 2:44 remaining.

An onside kick bounced Denver's way, and here's where things got interesting: both sides knew the stakes—if Denver scored a touchdown, the Broncos would be a two-point conversion from tying the game.

Tim led Denver steadily down the field, the tension rising with each play. The hometown crowd—who chanted "Tebow sucks!" in the first half—had changed their tune. Now they were screaming "Tebow! Tebow!" because many had seen him play so well in the clutch at Florida—and wanted to witness something special in Miami. The biggest play of the drive was a diving catch by Daniel Fells—good for 28 yards to the 3-yard line—with less than half a minute to play. On second down, Tim passed to Fells again for the touchdown. A two-point conversion would push

Tim punched in this touchdown during a Christmas Eve 2011 game against Buffalo—but that was one of the few highlights in a 40-14 loss to the Bills, who snapped a seven-game losing streak. (AP Photo/David Duprey)

the game into overtime.

Was there any doubt that Tim wanted the ball in his hands on the biggest play of the game? From the shotgun, he took the snap, saw a big hole to the right, and darted into the end zone untouched.

Miami won the overtime coin toss and elected to take the ball. But Broncos linebacker D.J. Williams soon stripped the ball from Dolphins quarterback Matt Moore. Three plays later, Matt Prater nailed a 51-yard field goal, and the jubilant Broncos players sprinted onto the field with their helmets held high. White-shirted Denver coaches jumped into each other's arms and bear-hugged. Everyone in the organization was celebrating on the sidelines like they had just won the Super Bowl on a final play.

Except for Tim. In the midst of the pandemonium, he dropped his right knee to the ground and started praying, worshipping the Lord of the Universe. Then he pointed his finger to the heavens.

We can't get into Tim's mind to know exactly what he communicated to God in those few moments, but I would imagine he was thanking the Lord for what had just happened.

Tim's moment was witnessed by millions watching on TV—and tens of millions more who would later see the clip of Tim genuflecting, offering a prayer of thanksgiving, then pointing to the sky in worship.

Among those watching the amazing comeback was Jared Kleinstein, a 24-year-old Denver native living in New York City. A half-dozen Denver expats were watching the game at Sidebar on East 15th when Jared noticed Tim taking a knee in prayer while his teammates jumped up and down. To commemorate the moment, Jared asked his friends to step outside the establishment, where he took a picture of them hunched down on one knee, their fists against their foreheads. Then, as young people do these days, he posted the photo on Facebook.

The "likes" poured in by the hundreds, which got him thinking. The following day, he created a "tebowing" blog on tumblr.com, then two days later purchased the *tebowing* domain name from GoDaddy.com and created a website.

Don't get the wrong idea: Kleinstein wasn't mocking Tim's act of supplication. In fact, on his splash page, he defined *tebowing* as a verb meaning to "get down on a knee and start praying, even if everyone else around is doing something completely different." Visitors to tebowing.com were invited to submit photos of others striking a tebowing pose.

How long did it take for the tebowing phenomenon to go viral? A day or two. Once the national news media got hold of the story, it seemed everyone was either tebowing or talking about it. Or submitting their random acts of tebowing to tebowing.com. There were pictures of

- an entire aisle of a 737 jet filled with passengers on one knee
- a bridal party—four groomsmen and four bridesmaids—tebowing while the just-married couple were locked in a kiss

- a college-aged tourist striking the pose with the Roman Colosseum in the background
- soldiers in Afghanistan tebowing in their camos
- the man himself—Tim Tebow—smiling next to a young Broncos fan who's tebowing on him

It's pretty cool how tebowing took on a life of its own, how people had fun with it without ridiculing Tim or his Christian faith.

The best part of the story: Jared Kleinstein is Jewish.

Tim, holding hands with Kansas City Chiefs outside linebacker Andy Studebaker during a post-game prayer time, doesn't look like a player on a team going to the NFL playoffs. Though the Broncos lost the last game of their regular season on January 2, 2012, they advanced to the post-season when the San Diego Chargers defeated the Oakland Raiders. (AP Photo/Jack Dempsey)

11
THE MILE HIGH MESSIAH

What happened in Miami made those who follow the NFL closely sit up and take notice: no team since the AFL-NFL merger in 1970 had ever won a game after trailing by 15 points or more with less than three minutes to play. Everyone, it seemed, was talking about the game. If Tim could snatch a victory like that from the jaws of defeat, the feeling was that he could do anything—like make the Broncos a winner again.

But here is where the Tim Tebow bus took a detour. In the very next game, a home contest against the hot Detroit Lions, Tim suffered through a humiliating afternoon. There were eight three-and-outs. A miserable 8-for-25 passing. An interception returned 100 yards for a coast-to-coast touchdown. Seven sacks. And at least two instances of on-the-field "tebowing" by Detroit players who *were* mocking the prayer pose.

The humbled Broncos stood at 2–5, and the question

thrown at Coach Fox was whether Tim would remain Denver's starting quarterback. I remember watching that game, feeling Tim looked overwhelmed by a massive pass rush that gave him very little time to find a receiver. Once again the social media chatter exploded in volume: *Tim Tebow is not an NFL quarterback. The pro game is too fast for him. He can't make the progressions.*

Coach Fox stayed the course, and it's good that he did—because that allowed Tebow fans to experience a wondrous six-game tear in which the Broncos won incredibly close games, often in the last series or in overtime. Most of the games were decided by a single touchdown or a field goal. Here's a recap:

- Against the Oakland Raiders—in the Black Hole—Denver fell behind 17–7 at the half, but Tim and the Broncos found their mojo and came roaring back. It wasn't until wide receiver Eddie Royal returned a punt 85 yards with six minutes to go in the game that Denver put their nose in front of their conference rival. Using the read-option like he was a magician, Tim either tucked the ball into the belly of running back Willis McGahee or kept it himself, punching out chunks of yards to keep the chains moving in the Broncos' 38–24 victory. Tim threw fewer times—only 21 attempts—but connected for two touchdowns. He was sacked only once after taking 13 in his first two games. Denver's record: 3–5.

- Tim threw even *fewer* times against Kansas City in Game 2 of the streak—only eight passes, with only two completions. But one of his passes—a beautiful deep ball that streaking Eric Decker caught over his shoulder—resulted in a 56-yard, fourth-quarter touchdown that was a dagger to the Chiefs' heart. The lightning strike put the Broncos ahead by 10 points in what would turn out to be a 17–10 victory. Denver's record: 4–5.

- The Broncos had just three days to prepare for their Thursday night game against the New York Jets in Denver. With a national audience watching on the NFL Network, Tim and the Broncos were backed up on the 5-yard line, down 13–10 late in the fourth quarter. Tim had struggled much of the game to find his rhythm. But with the game on the line, it was like Tim stepped out of a phone booth wearing a blue-and-orange Superman outfit. Running the read-option, spread offense to perfection, Tim led Denver down the field with his feet and his arm. Facing a third-and-four on the 20-yard line, the Jets threw an all-out blitz at Tim, who slipped off the left side and churned his legs toward the end zone for the game-winner. Final score: Denver 17, New York 13. Football pundits started calling him the "Mile High Messiah," and they had a point: Tim was taking a few measly fish and loaves of bread—his uneven play—and feeding the 5,000 in miraculous fashion with incredible last-minute comebacks. Denver's record: 5–5, exceeding their win total of 2010.

- Trailing 13–10 with just over five minutes to go in San Diego, Tim confidently marched the Broncos downfield for the tying field goal. Though it looked for awhile like neither team would score in overtime, resulting in a rare tie, Tim pushed Denver close enough for Matt Prater's 37-yard, game-winning kick with just 29 seconds left. Final score: Denver 16, San Diego 13. Denver's record: 6–5, one game behind Oakland.

- A road game in Minneapolis was Tim's next test. Denver started off slowly—what else is new?—but in the second half, the Broncos opened up the playbook. After intermission in the Metrodome, Tim showed he could sling with the best of them, completing six of nine passes for 173 yards and two touchdowns. He also earned a two-point conversion in the fourth quarter when he rolled to his right and found the goal line to tie the game at 29. Shades of Miami.

The wide-open second half felt like a shootout, but Tim and the Broncos still found themselves down by a field goal with three minutes to go. A 40-yard pass play got Denver within field goal range,

No one expected the Denver Broncos to beat the mighty Pittsburgh Steelers in the opening round of the 2012 NFL playoffs—which made victory taste that much sweeter. Here, Tim bear hugs his coach, John Fox, after the Broncos won 29-23 on the first play of overtime—an 80-yard touchdown strike from Tim to Demaryius Thomas. (AP Photo/Jack Dempsey)

and Matt Prater punched through a 46-yarder to knot the game again at 32. Then, with only 1:33 remaining, Tim watched Minnesota's rookie quarterback, Christian Ponder, make a horrible sideline pass that was intercepted deep in Viking territory. Tim ran the clock down before Mr. Automatic won it with a chip-shot field goal as time expired. Denver record: 7–5, now tied for first with the Raiders, who'd lost.

- The beat went on in Chicago, in the NFC's Black and Blue division. After a half of bruising football— and a rare scoreless tie—da Bears took a 10–0 lead early in the fourth quarter. But Tim started the comeback at the 4:34 mark, engineering a snappy seven-play drive that ended with a 10-yard touchdown pass to Demaryius Thomas. But with 2:08 to go, the Broncos were out of timeouts.

Unlike the Miami game, an onside kick didn't go Denver's way. It looked like Chicago would simply run the ball three times and punt; Denver might get the ball deep in its own territory with about 20 seconds to play. But Chicago running back Marion Barber made a mental mistake, allowing linebacker D.J. Williams to push him out of bounds. That meant an extra 40 seconds or so for Denver, which took a punt at 1:06 to start a final drive from their own 20, and advanced—on

Tebow passes to three different receivers—39 yards to the Chicago 41. Matt Prater's longshot 59-yard field goal attempt had enough leg to pass over the crossbar, forcing overtime. Of course.

Of course, the Bears' Marion Barber fumbled on the first possession of OT, with Chicago on Denver's 34-yard line, well within range of a game-winning field goal. Of course, Tim authored a heady, nine-play drive to *Chicago's* 34-yard line. Of course, Prater rocketed a 51-yard kick through the uprights for Tim's *sixth* game-winning drive in either the fourth quarter or overtime in his eleven starts.

Denver record: 8–5 after six straight wins, now first in the AFC West as Oakland lost again.

PATH TO THE PLAYOFFS

The Broncos were in the driver's seat. They controlled their own destiny. Win out, and they would ride a whole lot of momentum into the NFL playoffs.

One team they would expect to see in the postseason was New England, led by Tom Brady, considered by many the best quarterback in the game. And next on the regular-season schedule was the Patriots, in the Mile High City.

Rather untypically, Tim played great early to lead Denver to a 16–7 lead in the second quarter. But then it was *whoosh.* New England reeled off 27 unanswered points in annihilating the Broncos 41–23. The six-game streak was history.

Okay, no one was expecting this game in the W column

anyway. Buffalo, which had lost seven in a row, was coming up—so you'd have to think things were looking good.

Think again. The Bills throttled the Broncos, 40–14. Now it looked like the Broncos *had* to win their final regular season game against Kansas City to advance to the playoffs. And coming to Denver was none other than former Bronco starter Kyle Orton, waived a month earlier and picked up by the division rival Chiefs.

You can figure Orton had this game circled on his calendar.

The former Bronco quarterback didn't play spectacularly, but the Chiefs defense thwarted Tim and his offense the entire game, holding Denver to a single field goal in a 7–3 loss. But there was good news from Oakland, where the San Diego Chargers played spoiler with a 38–26 victory. Denver, Oakland, and San Diego each finished with 8–8 records, but Denver won the tiebreaker because of their better play against common opponents (5–5 for Denver; 4–6 for Oakland and San Diego).

Though the Broncos backed into the playoffs, they were a division winner—and would have home field advantage against Pittsburgh. The Steelers, who had finished just behind New England with a sterling 12–4 record, were heavily favored.

THE FOOTRACE TO THE END ZONE

If you like drama, you got nearly four hours of excitement in early January 2012.

The storyline going into the opening-weekend matchup was that the Steelers would steamroll the slumping Broncos because their "Steel Curtain" defense was arguably the toughest in the NFL. Besides, Tim's confidence had to be shot after losing the last three games of the regular season. Only the game's location—in Denver—would keep it from being a complete blowout.

But Pittsburgh had some issues, as well. Ben Roethlisberger, the sturdy-in-the-pocket passer, had suffered a high ankle sprain several weeks earlier and was far from 100 percent. Big Ben's howitzer arm still made him a dangerous threat, though.

In the lead-up to the big game, John Elway—the former Denver great—told a *Denver Post* columnist that Tim needed to "put everything behind him, go through his progressions, and pull the trigger."

Yes, sir.

Tim responded to the directive with one of his best passing games ever—and Denver's 20-point explosion in the second quarter was a thing of beauty. In addition to a pair of Matt Prater field goals, Tim lofted a handsome 30-yard pass to a well-covered Eddie Royal in the end zone and swiveled his hips on an eight-yard touchdown run of his own.

But you can never count Big Ben out—and by the force of his will and supreme talent, Roethlisberger brought the Steelers back from a two-touchdown deficit to force overtime. Denver won the toss . . . and everyone knows what happened next.

Following a touchback, on the first play of overtime, Tim strode to the line of scrimmage. The Steelers were showing a run-heavy front with nine men in the box, leaving a gaping hole in the middle. Then cornerback Ike Taylor crept up to the line,

In a playoff game in mid-January 2012, Tim was constantly pressured by a stout New England Patriots defense that kept him on the run. His counterpart, Tom Brady, stung the Broncos was five touchdown passes on the way to a one-sided 45-10 win. (AP Photo/David Drapkin)

where Demaryius Thomas had lined up split wide left.

Tim faked a handoff, then whistled a clean pass to Thomas, running a post pattern. The Denver wideout straight-armed Taylor and turned up the sideline with nothing but green real estate ahead. Turning on the afterburners, Thomas outran safety Ryan Mundy to the end zone.

Watching the play develop, Tim took off after Thomas, hoofing it to the end zone to celebrate with his delirious teammates.

"When I saw him scoring, first of all, I just thought, 'Thank you, Lord,'" Tim said. "Then I was running pretty fast, chasing him—like I can catch up to DT. Then I just jumped into the stands. First time I've done that. That was fun."

Tim's version of the Lambeau Leap—throwing his exhilarated body into the stands—had some fearing we'd never see him again. But he survived, and even had a spiritual moment amidst the hoopla. "Then I got on a knee and thanked the Lord again," Tim said, "and tried to celebrate with my teammates and the fans."

The 80-yard pass-and-catch was the longest scoring play in NFL overtime history. And it was the shortest overtime ever as well—only 11 seconds. Accolades poured in, and Tim was the toast of the NFL for the next week.

What I loved was that even some sports commentators caught the amazing coincidence that Tim threw for 316 yards, completing ten throws for an average of 31.6 yards per completion.

Guess what happened next? John 3:16 was the most popular Google search the following Monday.

THE END OF THE LINE

The top-seeded New England Patriots, who had smoked Denver just a month earlier, were waiting patiently after a first-round bye. They had plenty of motivation: much was made of the fact that the Bill Belichick-coached team had lost three consecutive playoff games, dating back to the 2008 Super Bowl XLII heartbreaker that ruined their supposed-to-be-first-ever 19–0 season.

In a highly anticipated Saturday night game, Tim and the Denver Broncos were taken out of the game early as Tom Brady threw *five* first-half touchdown passes. The Patriots coasted in the second half to an easy 45–10 victory. Tim wasn't much of a factor as a consistent pass rush either swallowed him up or caused him to throw away too many balls.

The magical mystery ride was over—but what a fascinating season of football. As they say sometimes, *You can't make this stuff up.*

That's certainly true of Tim Tebow's career. Considering the path he traveled—languishing on the sidelines in training camp, playing sketchy stretches of football, then conjuring up one amazing comeback after another—it makes you wonder if the Lord was having a little fun with football fans in America. But there was one more surprise lurking in the off-season.

Tim stayed busy with a series of appearances and speaking engagements. He attended Cartoon Network's Hall of Game Awards in Santa Monica, California, where he walked the green carpet with the likes of NBA icon Shaquille O'Neal, soccer star

David Beckham, and a bevy of pro athletes from other sports.

Asked on the green carpet what he thought of Jeremy Lin, the Asian-American, outspokenly Christian, overnight sensation with the New York Knicks, Tim replied, "I really like him. I respect him a whole lot. I've had the pleasure to really get to know him over the last few weeks. What a great guy he is. I just wish him the best of luck. How he handles himself and how he carries himself, I think he's a great role model. And I'm proud of him."

Tim was also approached to be on ABC's hit show *The Bachelor*. Personally, I couldn't see how hot tub hookups and Tim's stand for premarital purity would be a good match for the program . . . and Tim came through as I figured: "Haha rumors can be crazy!" he typed on his Twitter account. "Even though I've watched the show before, I'm definitely not gonna be on the Bachelor."

Then he had a "dinner date" with country music star Taylor Swift, who is certainly a cutie and just as famous as Mr. Tebow. But don't make too much of the tabloid fodder. Yes, the two dined at Toscanova Italian Restaurant in Los Angeles' Century City, but they were with William Morris agents—they're both represented by WME—so there's no way we can know why they were meeting or what they were discussing. Seems like they would make a nice couple, though . . .

And then there was a speaking engagement in Las Vegas, where Tim spoke about faith and football to 20,000 one weekend at Canyon Ridge Christian Church. During a Q&A time, when senior pastor Kevin Odor asked him about "tebowing," Tim showed him how to properly strike the prayerful pose on the church stage as the standing-room-only crowd howled.

"One of the reasons I get on a knee is because that's a form of humbling yourself," Tim explained. "I want to humble myself before the Lord and say thank you for this opportunity. Thank you for letting me play the game I love."

HIS LIFE TURNS UPSIDE DOWN

Following the 2011 season, the Indianapolis Colts had a big—and expensive—decision to make regarding their quarterback, Peyton Manning, widely viewed as one of the best signal callers in NFL history for his pinpoint passing and uncanny ability to read coverages. The team's most popular player, a Super Bowl winner, and four-time MVP, Manning had played his entire 14-year career in Indianapolis. He was the face of the Colts franchise. Well-liked. A pro's pro.

But Manning, sidelined by a series of neck surgeries, didn't play a down in the entire 2011 season. Without Old Reliable playing pitch and catch with his receivers, Indianapolis' record plummeted to 2–14, the worst in the NFL. The only good thing to come from the disastrous season was a guaranteed first pick in the 2012 NFL draft.

The Colts management had to decide whether to pick up the remaining four years on Manning's five-year, $90 million contract. If they did, that would mean paying an option bonus of $28 million on March 11, 2012. If the team released Manning, however, they could use that money to sign a new quarterback with their No. 1 draft pick—like Stanford University star Andrew Luck.

And so, with tears and fanfare, the Colts bid good-bye to Peyton Manning. All parties agreed it was a business decision: after all, Manning was turning 36 years old, had a creaky neck, and was due a ton of bonus money.

A dozen NFL teams inquired about being stops on the Peyton Manning Road Show. But it soon became apparent that only three were in serious contention—the Tennessee Titans, the San Francisco 49ers, and the Denver Broncos.

The news that the Broncos were interested in Manning—with John Elway leading the pursuit with the single-mindedness of a fourth-quarter drive—sent shock waves through the sporting universe. What about Tim Tebow? Hadn't he shown true grit with all those amazing late-game comebacks and leading the Broncos to a playoff win? Wasn't he responsible for changing the Broncos' culture of losing?

Sure he was. But since this was John Elway's rodeo, we'll never really know what the boss was thinking. We can figure that Manning felt very comfortable being wooed by Elway—they were kindred spirits, equals in the pantheon of great NFL quarterbacks. Elway probably said that he understood Manning's situation since he—Elway—had played quarterback at the same age. Elway had performed well, too, in his final act, winning Super Bowl rings when he was 37 and 38. Manning ultimately said yes to the Broncos, signing a $96 million, five-year contract.

Which meant Tim had to go. There was no way the Broncos organization or the coaching staff wanted the distraction that Tim would add to the mix, so Denver placed No. 15 on the trading block.

The New York Jets and the Jacksonville Jaguars stepped up with offers. The Jets had missed the playoffs in 2011, and fans and media seeking someone to blame cast their eyes on Mark Sanchez, the third-year quarterback who played poorly at times. Tim would give the Jets another option.

Jacksonville—Tim's hometown—certainly wanted to bring their favorite son back to Florida. Owner Shahid Khan, who had just completed his purchase of the Jaguars in January 2012, saw the value in having a guy like Tim Tebow on his team. Since the Jaguars had had attendance problems, Tim would fill up Ever-Bank Field and certainly give football fans in Florida something to talk about again. The Jags had a promising quarterback in Blaine Gabbert—but he hadn't set the world on fire in 2011.

In the end, Tim had a certain amount of say-so about the team he would play for. Exactly how much, we'll probably never know—but it was clear that Tim wanted to become a Jet, though he knew he was joining the team in a backup role. Perhaps he was thinking, deep down, that he could beat out Sanchez as the starting QB. And even if he didn't, he might push Sanchez to play better. Tim would do whatever he could to help the Jets win, whether that was running the Wildcat offense (where the guy taking the hike in short-yardage situations is expected to run the ball) or lining up at H-back to give the defense something else to think about.

But make no mistake about it—Tim has been and always will be a quarterback. That dream did not die when the Broncos showed him the door, and it won't die now that he wears a Jets uniform. And that's why the 2012 season will be such fun to watch. If Sanchez doesn't play up to par and the Jets lose a few games, it's a lock that frustrated fans at MetLife Stadium will chant "Tebow! Tebow!" just like they did in Denver.

So it's back to the future. Tim is starting over with a new team. He'd tell you that he's in New York for a reason, and it's all part of God's plan.

But who could have predicted this turn of events, especially after that magical 2011 season? But that's football—and Tim has always said the game comes in third on his list of priorities, after faith and family.

Just imagine, though, if he does get a chance—and makes the most of the opportunity. If the Jets pile up wins, they'll be talking about "Timsanity" in Gotham, much like Jeremy Lin touched off "Linsanity" during the strike-shortened NBA season.

So isn't it interesting that two of the most celebrated Christian athletes today find themselves in the center of the media universe, playing before an audience that literally numbers in the millions?

Let's pray that Tim will be remain humble and strong, stay free from injury, and continue to be a bold witness for Christ in the Big Apple. We can thank God that Tim has his football helmet screwed on straight, that he's a godly young man seeking to use his physical gifts for the glory of God.

Because this is a young man playing with purpose.

From the Mile High City to the Big Apple: Tim Tebow holds his first press conference with the New York Jets, who acquired him in a trade with the Denver Broncos in March 2012. (AP Photo/Mel Evans)

SOURCE MATERIAL

Introduction: He's Playing with Purpose in the Big Apple

"He's been called the NFL version's of a total solar eclipse . . ." "Fame, Fortune and Being Tim Tebow," by Johnette Howard, ESPN.com, April 22, 2010, and available at http://sports.espn.go.com/espn/commentary/news/story?page=howard/100422

"His agent, Jimmy Sexton, predicts Tim will become the best marketable athlete in history . . ." "Fame, Fortune and Being Tim Tebow," by Johnette Howard, ESPN. com, April 22, 2010, and available at http://sports.espn.go.com/espn/commentary/news/story?page=howard/100422

"The Davie-Brown Index . . ." "Not Even in NFL Yet, Tim Tebow Already a Marketing Trendsetter," Associated Press, April 19, 2010, and available at http://www.usatoday.com/sports/football/nfl/2010-04-19-tim-tebow-marketing_N.htm?utm_source=moggy&utm_medium=twitter&utm_campaign=GatorWire&utm_source=GatorWire&utm_medium=twitter&utm_campaign=MoggySocialMedia

1. In the Beginning

"Growing up, I knew my goal was to get a job and make a million dollars . . ." "Tebow's Family Vision Runs Much Deeper Than Just TDs," by Dave Curtis, *South Florida Sun-Sentinel*, August 8, 2008, and available at http://www.sunsentinel.com/sports/other/sfl-flsptebowdad08sbaug08,0,5446800.story

"Bob and Pam became friends, and their first date came a year after they met . . ." "Coaching Character," by Suzy A. Richardson, *Gainesville Sun,* October 7, 2007, and available at http://www.gainesville.com/article/ 20071007/NEWS/710060317?p=all&tc=pgall

"It wasn't always easy, but it was a wonderful time for our family . . ." "Coaching Character," by Suzy A. Richardson, *Gainesville Sun,* October 7, 2007, and available at http://www.gainesville. com/article/20071007/NEWS/710060317?p=all&tc=pgall

"I was weeping over the millions of babies being [aborted] in America . . ." "You Gotta Love Tim Tebow," by Austin Murphy, *Sports Illustrated,* July 27, 2009, and available at http://sportsillustrated.cnn.com/vault/article/ magazine/MAG1158168/index.htm

"Dysentery is common in developing and tropical countries like the Philippines. . ." "Amoebic Dysentery: How Common Is It?" the British Medical Journal Group in association with the *Guardian* newspaper, March 9, 2010, and available at http://www.guardian.co.uk/lifeandstyle/besttreatments/amoebic-dysenteryhow-common

"They didn't really give me a choice. That was the only option they gave me . . ." "Mothering Tebow," by Joni B. Hannigan, *Florida Baptist Witness*, January 8, 2009, and available at http://gofbw.com/News.asp?ID=9758

"It was amazing that God spared him, but we knew God had His hand on his life . . . " "Mothering Tebow," by Joni B. Hannigan, *Florida Baptist Witness*, January 8, 2009, and available at http://gofbw.com/News.asp?ID=9758

2. Back in the USA

"If I could get my kids to the age of 25 and they know God and serve God . . ." "Tebows to Headline Evangelism Conference Sessions," *Florida Baptist Witness*, January 29, 2008, and available at http://www.gofbw.com/news.asp?ID=8334

"But the Tebows *were* into competition . . ." "Competitive Fire Fuels Tebow," by Guerry Smith, Rivals.com Web site, December 8, 2007, and available at http://collegefootball.rivals.com/content.asp?cid=748732

"Some of his teammates were picking at the ground without even paying attention . . ." "Competitive Fire Fuels Tebow," by Guerry Smith, Rivals.com Web site, December 8, 2007, and available at http://collegefootball.rivals.com/content.asp?cid=748732

"One time, Tim wrote a report on why athletes' bodies need more protein . . ." "Pam Tebow's Labor of Love," by Lindsay H. Jones, *Denver Post*, May 10, 2010, and available at http://www.gainesville.com/article/20100510/ARTICLES/100519941?p=all&tc=pgall&tc=ar

"Guess that's my claim to fame . . ." "Tebow Caused a Stir Even as a Youngster," by Dave Curtis, *Orlando Sentinel*, December 5, 2007, and available at http://articles.orlandosentinel.com/2007-12-05/sports/tebowthekid05_1_quarterback-tim-tebow-hess-allen

3. Looking Up to a Hero

"That's not what Bob Tebow wanted for his son, though . . ." "Team Tebow," by Robbie Andreu, *Gainesville Sun*, January 31, 2006, and available at http://www.gainesville.com/article /20060131/GATORS01/201310351?p=all&tc=pgall&tc=ar

"We wanted to give Tim the opportunity to develop his God-given talent . . ." "Parents, High School Officials at Odds Over Motivation for Athletes' Transfers," by Ray Glier, *USA Today*, November 21, 2006, and available at http://www.usatoday.com/sports/preps/2006-11-21-transfers-cover_x.htm

"We were willing to make that sacrifice. We have made sacrifices for all our children . . ." "QB Facing College Challenges Grounded in Christ," by Barbara Denman, *Florida Baptist Witness*, January 17, 2006, and available at http://www.gofbw.com/news.asp?ID=5351

"People can always lead with words but not always with actions . . ." "A Gator for God," by Suzy Richardson, *Charisma*, October 2008, and available at http://www.charismamag.com/index.php/features/2008/october/17874-agator-for-god

"We had six road games my sophomore year . . ." "Tim Tebow Draws from High School Days at Nease," by Mitch Stephens at MaxPreps.com, February 16, 2010, and available at http://www.maxpreps.com/news/AmVWLhtREd-UswAcxJTdpg/tim-tebow-draws-from-high-school-daysat-nease.htm

4. The Green Shirt at Gator Nation

"Chris Leak is our quarterback . . . " "Orange Defeats Blue in a Less Than Spectacular Spring Finale," by Dennis Culver, *Gainesville Sun*, April 26, 2006, and available at http://www.gainesville.com/article/20060422/GATORS0108/60422003?p=all&tc=pgall

"There's room for another one next year, Timmy Tebow . . ." "Leak, Wuerffel Share Lifetime Gator Bond," by Pat Dooley, *Gainesville Sun*, January 14, 2007, and available at http://www.gainesville.com/article/20070114/GATORS24/70114040?p=all&tc=pgall&tc=ar

 "The story noted that Tim had sung 'She Thinks My Tractor's Sexy' . . . " "A Florida Folk Hero Prepares to Face Reality," by Pete Thamel, *New York Times*, September 1, 2007, and available at http://www.nytimes.com/2007/09/01/sports/ncaafootball/01florida.html?_r=1

"It makes you realize that everything that happens in this game doesn't really mean that much in the grand scheme of things . . ." "Notebook: UF's Tebow Takes Losses Hard, Gains Perspec-tive," by Brandon Zimmerman, *Gainesville Sun*, October 30, 2007, and available at http://www.gainesville.com/ar-ticle/20071030/NEWS/710300310?tc=ar

5. Promise Made, Promise Kept

"Tim took some hits from the media . . ." "John 3:16—Latest Bible Verse to Be Featured on Tim Tebow's Eye Black," by Tom Herrera, *NCAA Football Fanhouse*, January 9, 2009, and available at http://ncaafoot-ball.fanhouse.com/2009/01/09/john-3-16-latest-bible-verse-to-be-featured-on-tim-tebow/

"He's just an amazing young man, an amazing football player . . ." "Tebow Wins Wuerffel Award," by Robbie Andreu, *Gainesville Sun*, December 9, 2008, and available at http://www.gainesville.com/article/20081209/NEWS/812090943

"You knew he was going to lead us to victory . . ." "Tebow Engineers Comeback," by Kevin Brockway, *Gainesville Sun*, December 7, 2008, and available at http://www.gainesville.com/article/20081207/NEWS/812060925

"I was pretty excited . . . " "Best Player Ever? I'll Take Tebow" by Pat Dooley, *Gainesville Sun*, January 9, 2009, and available at http://www.gainesville.com/article/20090109/COLUMNISTS/901090279?p=all&tc=pgall&tc=ar

7. Plenty of Predraft Drama

" 'It's simple,' said one NFL scout . . ." "Tim Tebow Senior Bowl: Disaster or First Step to NFL?" by Mark Sappenfield, *Christian Science Monitor*, January 31, 2010, and available at http://www.csmonitor.com/USA/Society/2010/0131/Tim-Tebow-Senior-Bowl-Disaster-or-first-step-to-NFL

"Scouts Inc. gave Tim a D+ grade . . ." "2010 Senior Bowl: Tim Tebow's Performance Adds to His Plummeting NFL Draft Stock," by Daniel Wolf, Bleacher Report.com, January 30, 2010, and available at http://bleacherreport.com/articles/336387-tim-tebow-senior-bowl-performanceadds-to-plummeting-nfl-draft-stock

"No mention of abortion . . . because they were a division winner" "Tim Tebow's Brilliant Fake Leads to Pro-Life Score," by David Gibson, PoliticsDaily.com, February 7, 2007, and available at http://www.politicsdaily.com/2010/02/07/tim-tebows-brilliant-fake-leads-to-pro-life-score/

8. Combine Time

"It's more of a tweak . . ." "Tim Tebow's New Team Honing His Technique," by Sam Farmer, *Los Angeles Times*, February 27, 2010, and available at http://articles. latimes.com/2010/feb/27/sports/la-sp-nfl-combine27-2010feb27

"Kurt Hester, the corporate director of training at D1 . . ." "What's It Like to Help Tim Tebow Prepare for the NFL? D1's Kurt Hester Is Here to Tell You," by Ben Volin, *Palm Beach Post*, February 22, 2010, and available at http://blogs. palmbeachpost.com/gatorbytes/2010/02/22/whats-it-like-to-helptim-tebow-prepare-for-the-nfl-d1s-kurt-hester-is-here-to-tell-you/

"For all the television time, Internet bandwidth . . ." "Florida's Pro Day Was a True Circus, with Tim Tebow Front and Center," by Andy Staples, SI.com, March 18, 2010, and available at http://sportsillustrated.cnn.com/2010/writers/andy_staples/03/17/tim.tebow.pro.day/index.html

"The 15 minutes passed by way too quickly . . ." "Tebow Quickly Impressed McDaniels, Broncos as a Genuine Gem," by Lindsay H. Jones, *The Denver Post*, April 25, 2010, and available at http://www.denverpost.com/broncos/ci_14953999

9. The 2010 NFL Draft

"When quarterbacks Peyton Manning and Ryan Leaf were in the running . . ." "Leaf's Pro Career: Short and Unhappy," by Damon Hack, *New York Times*, August 4, 2002, and available at http://www.nytimes.com/2002/08/04/sports/profootball-leaf-s-pro-career-short-and-unhappy.html

"It would have been exciting to be here . . ." "Tebow Declines Invitations to Attend Draft, Decides to Return Home," by Jason La Canfora, NFL.com, April 21, 2010, and available at http://www.nfl.com/draft/story?id=09000d5d817aa5ce&template=with-video-withcomments&confirm=true

"Tim's former teammate at Florida, Cincinnati Bengals wide receiver Andre Caldwell . . ." "Bengals' Andre Caldwell: Right Spot to Pick Tim Tebow Is 'Late Second Round,'" *USA Today*'s The Huddle, March 31, 2010, and available at http://content.usatoday.com/communities/thehuddle/post/2010/03/bengals-andrecaldwell-right-spot-to-pick-tim-tebow-is-late-second-round/1

"Miami Dolphins quarterback Chad Henne . . ." "Dolphins' Chad Henne on Tim Tebow: 'He's Not an NFL Quarterback,' " *USA Today*'s The Huddle, March 18, 2010, and available at http://content.usatoday.com/communities/thehuddle/post/2010/03/dolphins-chad-henne-hes-not-annfl-quarterback/1

" . . . Tim did an interview on ESPN Radio with host Freddie Coleman . . ." "Time Tebow Does Not Take Mel Kiper's Criticism Kindly, Calls Him Out on Air," by Will Brinson, NCAA Football Fanhouse, December 19, 2008, and available at http://ncaafootball.fanhouse.com/2008/12/19/tim-tebow-does-not-takemel-kipers-criticism-kindly-calls-him/

"On the morning of the NFL draft . . . " "Tim Tebow: Is He a Miracle Worker, or Just an Average QB?" by Jon Saraceno, *USA Today*, April 22, 2010, and available at http://www.usatoday.com/sports/football/nfl/2010-04-21-tim-tebow_N.htm

"If you want Tim to be on your football team . . ." "Great Tebow Draft Debate Will Finally Be Answered," by Robbie Andreu, *Gainesville Sun*, April 21, 2010, and available at http://www.gainesville.com/article/20100421/ARTICLES/100429878?p=all&tc=pgall&tc=ar

"Kiper and his ESPN sidekick, Todd McShay, stuck to their guns . . ." "Great Tebow Draft Debate Will Finally Be Answered," by Robbie Andreu, *Gainesville Sun*, April 21, 2010, and available at http://www.gainesville.com/article/20100421/ARTICLES/100429878?p=all&tc=pgall&tc=ar

"And that's when Tim's cell phone rang with a 303 area code . . ." "Tim Tebow Drafted by Denver Broncos in First Round of NFL Draft," by Jeremy Fowler, *South Florida Sun-Sentinel,* April 23, 2010, and available at http://articles.sun-sentinel.com/2010-04-23/sports/sfl-tim-tebow-broncos-10_1_tim-tebow-25th-selection-later-round

"Coach McDaniels was on the line, but he didn't seem at all in a hurry . . ." "Mile-High on Tebow," by Robbie Andreu, *Gainesville Sun*, April 23, 2010, and available at http://www.gainesville.com/article/20100423/ARTICLES/4231012?p=all&tc=pgall&tc=ar

"I just think I showed them [the Broncos] I was willing to do whatever it took . . ." "Tim Tebow Drafted by the Denver Broncos," Alligator Army website, April 22, 2010, and available at http://www.alligatorarmy.com/2010/4/22/1437123/tim-tebow-drafted-by-the-denver

"Tim Tebow is a lightning rod . . ." "Colorado Evangelicals Singing Praises of McDaniels' QB Pick Tebow," by Electa Draper, *The Denver Post*, April 24, 2010, and available at http://www.denverpost.com/news/ci_14948943

10. Rookie Year

"Tim needs to work on the fundamentals of being a pocket passer . . ." "Elway Says Young QB Tebow Needs Work as a Pocket Passer," by Lindsay H. Jones, *The Denver Post*, January 6, 2011, available at http://www.denverpost.com/broncos/ci_17021315

"Most people wait until they're at least 24 . . ." "Tim Tebow Shows Charisma on MSNBC's Morning Joe," *Orlando Sentinel*, June 3, 2011, and available at http://blogs.orlandosentinel.com/sports-sentinel-sports-now/2011/06/03/tim-tebow-shows-charisma-on-msnbcs-morning-joe-video/

"Nice kid, sincere as a first kiss . . ." "Tim Tebow Not Ready for Prime Time," by Rick Reilly, espn.com, August 9, 2011, and available at http://espn.go.com/espn/story/_/id/6846531/tim-tebow-not-ready-prime-time

"He makes plays, you can't deny that . . ." "Chargers Hold Off Tebow-Inspired Broncos, 29-24," Associated Press, October 9, 2011, and available at http://sportsillustrated.cnn.com/football/nfl/gameflash/2011/10/09/4472_recap.html

11. The Mile High Messiah

"Tim needed to 'put everything behind him' . . ." "John Elway Has Advice for Tim Tebow," Associated Press, January 5, 2012, and available at http://goo.gl/SaZaF

"When I saw him scoring . . ." "Behind Tebow's Magic, Broncos Stun Steelers in Overtime Thriller," by CBS Channel 4 Denver, January 8, 2012, and available at http://denver.cbslocal.com/2012/01/08/broncos-stun-steelers-in-overtime-thriller/

"I really like him . . . " "Jeremy Lin + Tim Tebow = Cutest Sports Bromance Ever," by Jill Baughman, Cafemom.com, February 23, 2012, and available at http://thestir.cafemom.com/sports/133481/jeremy_lin_tim_tebow_cutest

"One of the reasons I get on a knee . . ." "Tebow's Appearance at Vegas Church Draws 20,000," Associated Press, March 5, 2012, and available at http://lasvegas.cbslocal.com/2012/03/05/tebows-appearance-at-vegas-church-draws-20000/

ABOUT THE AUTHOR

Mike Yorkey, a former *Focus on the Family* magazine editor and author or co-author of more than seventy books, has written about sports all his life for a variety of publications, including *Breakaway, Brio, Tennis, Skiing,* and *City Sports* magazines.

His most recent sports book is *Playing with Purpose: Inside the Lives and Faith of the Major League's Top Players* (with Jesse Florea and Joshua Cooley), which released with the start of the 2012 baseball season. He also authored *Playing with Purpose: Inside the Lives and Faith of Top NBA Stars* as well as a new biography—called *Linspired*—about Jeremy Lin, the first Asian-American player of Chinese-Taiwanese descent to play in the NBA.

Mike is also the co-author of *Every Man's Battle* with Steve Arterburn and Fred Stoeker and is a novelist who, with Tricia Goyer, co-authored the World War II thriller *Chasing Mona Lisa,* which was released in 2012.

Mike and his wife, Nicole, are the parents of two adult children, Andrea and Patrick. They make their home in Encinitas, California.

Mike's website is www.mikeyorkey.com.

For more great stories of
faith in sport,
check out the
Playing with Purpose
Series!

PLAYING WITH PURPOSE: BASKETBALL

Meet the "dream team" of talented NBA players with fascinating faith stories, including 2012 sensation Jeremy Lin of the New York Knicks. ISBN 978-1-61626-489-5

PLAYING WITH PURPOSE: BASEBALL

Meet the "starting lineup" of talented major league players with fascinating faith stories, including Albert Pujols, Josh Hamilton, Mariano Rivera, and 2011 Cy Young Winner Clayton Kershaw. ISBN 978-1-61626-490-1

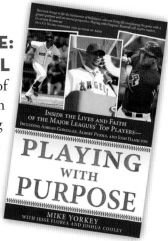

Available wherever Christian books are sold.